IMMORTAL MENTOR

IMMORTAL MENTOR

KIRK ANTHONY FORD

INTRODUCTION

In the shadowed corners of human understanding, a question lingers, heavy with the breath of millennia: Can the essence of life itself be not just extended, but rendered unending? Herein lies our conundrum, a puzzle that has ensnared philosophers and prophets alike. Why has the promise of immortality, so clearly inscribed in ancient texts, been left to gather dust in the recesses of our collective consciousness? Picture a world where the finality of death is but a faint whisper, overrun by the resounding echo of eternal life. Have we, as seekers of truth and wisdom, fallen prey to our own limitations, our vision clouded by a lack of revelation? Why do we falter at the threshold of immortality, our steps unsure? Could it be that the key has always been within our grasp, hidden in plain sight, waiting for the illu-mination of genuine wisdom to reveal its potency? It is a baptism of fire, a Mantle of Sonship, bestowed upon us, yet scarcely claimed. What if I told you that immortality is not a distant dream, but a present reality, an unfolding revelation through the gospel? As the pages turn, a narrative unfolds, one that beckons you to step beyond the veil of the temporal, to embrace a truth so profound, that it has the power to reshape the very fabric of existence. But dare we wield such knowledge, to become the heirs of an immortal legacy? The path lies before us, fraught with the unknown, and it is here, at the precipice of discovery, that I must leave you... on the cusp of eternity.

In a world teeming with fleeting pleasures and ephemeral joys, the human heart yearns for something more enduring, a promise of permanence amidst the relentless tide of time. This yearning is as old as humanity itself, a deep-seated desire that has driven the greatest quests and defined the noblest pursuits. Yet, despite our advancements, the riddle of eternal life remains unsolved, an enigma wrapped in the shrouds of our finite understanding. It is this very riddle that I, Kirk Anthony, aim to unravel through the pages of "Immortal Mentor."

Our society, rich in knowledge and technological prowess, stands at a crossroads, where the ancient paths of wisdom seem overgrown by the weeds of modern skepticism. We pride ourselves on our intellectual achievements, yet we have failed to grasp the full magnitude of the life-giving truths that have been gifted to us. There is a Mantle of Sonship, a divine legacy, that has been offered to all of humanity, yet it lies unclaimed, like a treasure locked away in a chest for which we have misplaced the key.

The impact of our collective oversight is profound. We live in the shadows of mortality, our days numbered, our aspirations shackled by the looming specter of death. The vibrant colors of life are dulled by the inevitability of decay, and the beauty of our experiences is tainted by the certainty of their end. We are, in essence, a race running a race against time, never quite able to savor the fullness of our existence, for the dread of its conclusion haunts our every step.

And yet, within this bleak landscape, there are those who have glimpsed a different reality, a hint of the immortal. I recall a story that stirred my soul to its very core—a tale of a man who had been touched by the divine, who had seen beyond the veil of this temporal realm. At the tender age of nine, while wandering the icy expanses of Alaska, he was visited by a figure of radiant light, a being who spoke of life beyond the bounds of death. This man, whom I have the privilege of knowing intimately, was none other than myself, and the encounters that followed at 23, 25, and 27 only served to cement the truth that had been revealed to me.

The stakes could not be higher. The very essence of our existence hangs in the balance, the possibility of a life unencumbered by the fear of death. To ignore the call to immortality is to resign ourselves to a cycle of birth and decay, to forsake the gift that has been so lavishly offered to us. But to heed the call is to step into a realm of boundless potential, to live fully and without regret, with the knowledge that our story does not end with the final breath.

As we embark on this journey together, let me offer you a glimpse of the path that lies ahead. Through the wisdom of the gospel, as revealed in the writings of apostles and prophets, and illuminated by the light of 2 Timothy 1:9-10, we will explore the contours of this Mantle of Sonship. This Baptism of Fire, once witnessed in the Son of God within the fiery furnace, is not a mere metaphor, but a tangible reality that can be experienced in the here and now.

"Immortal Mentor" is not just another book; it is a call to awaken, rise from the ashes of our limited understanding, and embrace the fullness of life promised to us. It is a guide, a map to the buried treasure of immortality that awaits those brave enough to seek it. With each chapter, we will peel back the layers of mystery that have shrouded this truth, bringing to light the revelations that have the power to transform the very essence of what it means to be human.

So, I invite you, dear reader, to join me on this quest for the immortal, to dare to believe in the incredible, and to open your heart to the profound possibilities that await. Together, we will uncover the secrets long forgotten, and step boldly into the promise of an unending tomorrow.

Are you ready to take the first step? Can you feel the stirrings of eternity within your soul? The journey of a thousand lifetimes begins with the turn of a page...

Welcome to "Immortal Mentor."

1

THE GENESIS OF IMMORTALITY

The Immortal Blueprint

The Book of the GENERATION of Jesus Christ, the son of David, the son of Abraham. (Matthew 1:1, KJV)

Generation in Greek is the word "GENESIS." Jesus is the REGENERATION or The Genesis of Life and Immortality!

At the heart of every human endeavor lies the search for meaning, for a purpose that transcends the ordinary, grounding our fleeting existence in something eternal. It is this quest that has led us to the doorsteps of history's greatest teacher, whose words echo through time with the promise of life unending. The teachings of Jesus of Nazareth, illuminated in the sacred scriptures, offer not just solace but a blueprint for immortality—a path laid out with the precision of a master craftsman.

The central theme of this journey is no less than the secret to eternal life, a blueprint sketched in the dust of ancient roads and inscribed upon the hearts of those who would follow. To understand this mystery, we delve into the core teachings of Jesus, teachings that are both a promise and a meticulous process.

The main assertion of our exploration is bold, yet it stands firmly upon the foundation of historical and theological scrutiny: Jesus proffered a blueprint for immortality, a series of steps and principles that, if embraced and enacted, could lead to life everlasting.

Our primary evidence for such a claim can be found within the Beatitudes, the poetic and profound statements Jesus shared during the Sermon on the Mount. Here, he outlined the attitudes and behaviors that align with the kingdom of heaven—a kingdom not limited by the constraints of temporal existence. "Blessed are the pure in heart, for they shall see God," he proclaimed, linking the purification of one's inner life with the vision of the eternal.

We must delve deeper into the evidence, examining each Beatitude as a component of this blueprint. The call to humility, to hunger and thirst for righteousness, to be merciful, to be peacemakers—each of these pronouncements carries with it the weight of eternal implications. To embody these virtues is to align oneself with the divine nature, a nature that knows no end.

Yet, there are counter-evidence and counterarguments aplenty. Critics argue that the Beatitudes are idealistic at best, impossible standards that serve only to highlight human frailty. They contend that immortality, as a concept, is a myth, a comforting narrative crafted to ease the sting of our inevitable demise.

In rebuttal, we return to the very source of our claim, the scriptures themselves, which offer numerous accounts of individuals who encountered the divine and were transformed. Consider the tale of Lazarus, brought back from the dead, a story that illustrates the power over mortality Jesus claimed to possess and impart to others.

Additional supporting evidence lies in the practices of the early Christian community. Their radical commitment to the teachings of Jesus, even in the face of death, suggests they had tapped into a source of life that transcended their earthly trials. Their unwavering faith serves as a testament to the transformative power of the blueprint before us.

As we reach the conclusion of this chapter, we reinforce the assertion that Jesus laid out a blueprint for immortality. The evidence is manifold, found in the Beatitudes, the miracles, and the lives of the early disciples. Each element points to a process that is as practical as it is profound, promising a life that stretches beyond the horizon of death.

So, we stand at the threshold of understanding, gazing into the depths of a promise that has captivated the hearts of generations. The blueprint is before us, intricate and inviting. Dare we take up the tools provided and build upon the foundation laid by the Immortal Mentor? Can we embody the principles that promise not just life, but life everlasting?

The journey is arduous, the path steeped in mystery. Yet, with each step forward, we move closer to the realization of a dream as old as time itself. The Immortal Blueprint is not just a set of teachings; it is an invitation to step into a reality where death has lost its sting, and life, in all its fullness, beckons us onward.

Are you prepared to embrace this journey? Will you let the ancient words take root in your heart and guide you to a destiny that defies the grave? The choice lies before you, an open door to a realm where the immortal heart beats strong, undimmed by the shadows of mortality.

Welcome to the next chapter of "Immortal Mentor." The blueprint awaits.

Sonship Defined

Understanding sonship, particularly in the realm of immortality, requires a foray into a lexicon rich with meaning and history. These terms are not mere words; they are the lifeblood of a profound concept that has traversed time, shaping legacies and destinies.

Embarking on this exploration, it becomes evident why the unveiling of these terms is not just beneficial but essential. For without a firm grasp on the language of sonship, one might as well be adrift in an ocean of wisdom without a compass. It is with this understanding that we begin to parse the sacred vocabulary of eternal lineage.

To navigate these waters, we introduce a lexicon of the most pivotal terms: "Sonship," "Immortality," "Mentorship," "Legacy," and "Transfiguration." Each word is a pillar supporting the grand edifice of our discussion.

Sonship, the cornerstone of our exploration, is more than biological lineage. It is the conscious adoption of a mentor's values, virtues, and vision. When we speak of the sonship of the immortal, we refer not to the perpetuation of genetic material but to the continuation of ideals and wisdom that surpass the boundaries of mortality.

Immortality, often misconstrued as mere unending existence, in truth, embodies the essence of a life that is imperishable in value, influence, and manifestation. It is the enduring impact of a life well-lived, one that resonates through the ages and inspires the living while entering within the veil.

Mentorship, in this sacred context, is not a simple transfer of knowledge. It is the careful cultivation of another's potential, guiding them toward their own path of enlightenment and immortality.

Legacy is the imprint left upon the sands of time, a tapestry woven from one's actions, teachings, and the lives touched. It is what survives us, the story told in our stead, and the light we kindle in others that burns beyond our final breath.

Lastly, Transfiguration is the journey beyond the ordinary, the ascent to a higher state of being and understanding. It is the ultimate goal of sonship and the heart of immortality.

Mentorship, too, finds its reflection in the world around us. The relationship between Elijah and Elisha, Jesus and the Apostles, Andrew Carnegie and Doctor Napoleon Hill, President Barack Obama, and President Joe Biden, exemplifies a mentorship that shaped culture itself. Jesus's works carry the voice of his immortal mentorship into our present, a testament to the power of shared wisdom.

Legacy is evident in the foundations laid by pioneers and visionaries. Martin Luther King Jr.'s dream of equality and justice did not perish with him; it continues to inspire action and change, a legacy that transcends his temporal life.

Transfiguration is the pursuit that drives individuals to scale the peaks of human limitations. It is the spirit that propelled humankind to the moon, not merely as a physical feat but as a leap into a broader understanding of our place in the cosmos. If we can get to the moon what about mentorship from the sun (Matthew 17:2)?

As we draw this exploration to a close, let us reflect on the profound weight each term carries. These are not just definitions; they are the threads that weave the fabric of a concept that has, does, and will continue to shape the human narrative. Sonship, in the context of immortality, is an ever-unfolding story, a mantle passed down through the ages, inviting each of us to take up the charge and extend the lineage of wisdom and virtue into an eternal future.

The discourse on sonship does not end here; it is merely a pause, a moment to gather the threads before weaving them into the larger tapestry of 'Immortal Mentorship'. The journey continues, and with each step, the definitions provided here will illuminate the path, guiding us deeper into the mysteries of eternal life and legacy.

Are these concepts merely philosophical constructs, or do they hold tangible significance in your life? As you ponder this, consider the immortality of your actions, the mentorship you might provide, and the legacy you are crafting at this very moment.

The Mantle in Action

In the hush of twilight, a gentle breeze whispered through the olive trees of ancient Jerusalem, carrying with it the soft, earnest voices of two men deep in conversation. The younger man, a devoted student, hung on every word of his teacher, a prophet whose wisdom seemed as boundless as the stars beginning to pierce the dusky sky. This was no ordinary exchange; it was the passing of a mantle, the sacred sonship of spiritual lineage being lovingly draped over-eager, waiting shoulders.

The teacher, known to us through the annals of history as the prophet Elijah, was a figure of such fiery faith and miraculous power that his very presence seemed to alter the atmosphere. By his side was Elisha, a young man whose resolute gaze betrayed his determination to inherit not just the cloak that would soon fall from Elijah's ascension, but also the depth of character and divine purpose that his mentor embodied.

As they walked and talked, Elisha's heart raced with an anticipation that eclipsed fear. He knew this night would change everything. Elijah's narrative had been punctuated by the spectacular—raising the dead, calling down fire from heaven, outrunning chariots. And now, Elisha stood on the cusp of stepping into a story that would intertwine with his own, a narrative of divine mentorship culminating in a chariot of fire and horses of flame.

Can you imagine the surge of emotion in that sacred moment? The longing for a double portion of Elijah's spirit, the raw yearning for a legacy that would outlive the mortal coil? Elisha's journey was laden with the unexpected, a testament to the unpredictable nature of carrying the mantle. Yet, it was a journey that would cement his place in the continuum of divine sonship.

Fast forward several millennia, and the mantle of mentorship continues to cascade through time, reaching modern shores with undiminished power. In the heart of Honolulu, a young man named Kirk finds himself grappling with the weight of his own inheritance. An Air Force veteran, highly decorated, and a summa cum laude graduate, he was no stranger to discipline and excellence. Yet, his encounter with the Divine at the tender age of nine had set him on a path that no military precision or academic accolade could have prepared him for.

Kirk's story, much like Elisha's, is one of unexpected turns. Sent to Hawaii from Alaska, he encountered Jesus not once but several times throughout his life, each encounter molding him into a vessel ready to receive and pass on the mantle of heavenly wisdom. It was in these encounters that the mantle of sonship was extended to him, a mantle that he now stretches out to others as a mentor in faith and life.

What lessons can we draw from these narratives of ancient prophets and contemporary warriors? What universal truths do they unveil?

The mantle of sonship is a call to a higher purpose, a beckoning to embrace a legacy that transcends our finite existence. It is the baton in an eternal relay, passed from one generation to the next, each runner striving to carry it with honor and pass it on with even greater fervor.

But what does it mean for you, the reader? Are you ready to grasp the edge of the mantle as it flutters within reach, wrap it around your shoulders, and accept the responsibility that comes with it? For within these pages lies wisdom hard-won through both revelation and resilience. The anecdotes shared here, the stories of Elijah and Elisha, Kirk, and countless others, serve as gateways to a deeper comprehension of the divine mentorship that is offered to each of us.

The insights you stand to gain are manifold. They are insights of courage and conviction, of divine encounters that defy explanation yet demand a response. They are revelations of a mentorship that shapes lives, molds destinies, and forges legacies of imperishable influence. In embracing the mantle of sonship, you too can step into a role that has the potential to echo through the ages.

So I ask you, dear reader, are you prepared to journey into the heart of this immortal mentorship? To delve into the depths of a legacy that will outlast the stars? The mantle is before you, and the choice is yours. Will you let it pass by, or will you seize it with both hands and step into the fullness of your calling?

The story continues, and it beckons you to become a part of its unfolding mystery. The mantle is in action, and it awaits your response.

A Glimpse of Transfiguration

In the quietude of a world that never ceases its relentless spin, there lies a moment captured in the ancient texts that pierce the veil between temporal existence and the eternal. This, the event of the Mount Transfiguration, stands as a beacon, illuminating the path of spiritual metamorphosis and beckoning the spirit, soul, and body toward the undying light of immortality.

On a mountain high and removed from the clamor of worldly concerns, a figure known to us as Jesus underwent a transformation so profound that it defies simple comprehension. With him, Peter, James, and John witnessed what can only be described as a glimpse into the very essence of divine glory. The visage of Jesus shone like the sun, his garments became dazzling white, and the prophets Moses and Elijah appeared in conversation with him.

Why draw a parallel between this transcendent occurrence and the concept of spiritual metamorphosis? To understand this, one must first grasp the significance of the figures involved. Jesus, as the embodiment of divine mentorship, represents the ultimate guide on the journey to immortality. Moses, the giver of the Law, and Elijah, the prophet of fire and zeal, symbolize the foundational pillars of faith—law and prophecy which within Kirk's mantle, introduces these same pillars of law, prophetic tonsure of life and immortality through Sonship. Their presence alongside the transfigured

Jesus underscores the fulfillment of a divine promise, the amalgamation of history, and the ushering in of a new covenant.

The purpose of juxtaposing the Mount Transfiguration with the spiritual journey of an individual is to reveal the transformation that awaits the seeker of truth. It is an invitation to consider the process of inner change that leads to a life beyond the mere physical, a life marked by a profound connection with the divine.

The criteria for this comparison rest upon the transformative experiences of the soul: encounters with the divine, moments of profound realization, and the resultant change in one's way of being. The Mount Transfiguration serves as a template, a mystical mirror in which we may view the potential for our own spiritual and immortal transfiguration.

In their similarities, both the event on the mountain and the journey of the soul involve an unveiling, an exposure to a reality that lies beyond the ordinary. Just as Jesus revealed his divine nature to his disciples, so too does the seeker of immortality experience revelations that reshape their understanding of existence. Both are accompanied by a sense of awe, a recognition of something greater at work, and a call to a deeper communion with the sacred.

Yet in contrast, while the Transfiguration was a singular, historical event, the path of spiritual and immortal metamorphosis is an ongoing process, one that unfolds uniquely within each individual. The disciples were passive witnesses to Jesus' transformation, whereas the seekers actively participated in their own spiritual evolution.

Visual aids, though not present in the traditional sense, could be represented by the contrasting imagery of the mountain and the valley. The mountain is a place of revelation and divine encounter, versus the valley, where life's trials and day-to-day struggles take place. The stark differences in these terrains reflect the highs and lows of the spiritual journey.

The insights gleaned from this analysis are profound. The Transfiguration reveals that spiritual and immortal metamorphosis is not merely an internal shift but one that can manifest outwardly, influencing one's presence and impact on the world. It suggests that immortality is not a static state but a dynamic process of becoming more aligned with the divine essence.

In contemporary relevance, the quest for immortality might not involve physical mountains, but it does require overcoming the metaphorical mountains of doubt, fear, and complacency. The event of the Transfiguration stands as an enduring testament that such a transformation is not only possible but is the very goal of the spiritual journey.

So, what does this mean for you, the reader, in your quest for eternal wisdom? How does the story of a mountain, a man transfigured, speak to your heart in the here and now? Can you feel the pull of that sacred event, the call to rise above the mundane and behold the face of the everlasting?

It is here, in the contemplation of these profound mysteries, that one might find the keys to unlock the door to an existence marked by the divine. The journey is long, the climb is steep, and the process is arduous. Yet, the promise of transformation, of becoming more than what we are, whispers in the winds that sweep down from that ancient summit.

The mantle of sonship, the quest for immortality, the yearning for a touch of the infinite—these are not relics of a bygone era but living, breathing realities that beckon each of us forward. The Transfiguration is not simply a story to be read but a reality to be lived. Will you, then, take this glimpse of transfiguration and allow it to reshape your own journey toward the immortal?

As the pages of this book turn, as the words etch themselves upon your spirit, consciousness, and body, may you find within them the courage to embrace the path of transformation. The mantle awaits, the mountain calls, and the journey to immortality continues. Will you climb?

Voices of Calling

The air was thick with the scent of salt and the rhythmic sound of waves crashing against the rugged Hawaiian shoreline. A young man, head bowed in silent contemplation, sat upon the sun-warmed rocks, his thoughts as tumultuous as the ocean before him. His name was Kirk, a name that, in a past life, was synonymous with the honor of a highly decorated Air Force veteran, the prestige of a collegiate Summa Cum Laude graduate, and the distinction of being a member of the Delta Mu Delta Scholastic Honor Society for Business. Yet, at this moment, titles and accolades bore no weight. Kirk was simply a man wrestling with a call that transcended the very fabric of his being.

As the last vestiges of sunlight dipped below the horizon, painting the sky in hues of fiery orange and somber purple, Kirk's mind wandered back to his ninth year, to an encounter that would forever alter the course of his life. It was a moment of divine interjection, a sudden and unexpected meeting with Jesus that left an indelible mark on his soul. The memory was as vivid as the day it happened, the presence of the divine as real as the rocks he sat upon.

The years that followed brought with them additional encounters—at twenty-three, then twenty-five, and again at twenty-seven—each one a stepping stone on the path of sonship to which he had been called. These were not mere moments of clarity or fleeting spiritual highs; they were profound experiences that demanded a response, a complete surrender to a journey both daunting and sacred.

But what was it about this call to sonship that seemed to resonate deep within the chambers of every heart? Why did it stir souls to their core and beckon them toward a destiny that felt simultaneously foreign and familiar?

Kirk's gaze fell upon a small family playing at the water's edge, their laughter a soothing balm to his contemplative spirit. In the innocence of a child's joy, he saw reflected the universal nature of yearning, the innate desire to belong, to be part of something greater. Suddenly, it dawned on him that the call to sonship was not his alone to bear; it was a universal anthem, a song sung since the dawn of creation, inviting all to partake in the divine dance of eternity.

Is it not true that within each of us lies the potential for greatness, the ability to transcend the ordinary and touch the hem of the extraordinary? Kirk pondered, his heart swelling with an emotion that was as raw as it was real.

As night descended and the first stars began to twinkle in the firmament, Kirk felt a peace settle over him. It was as if the universe itself was whispering secrets, revealing the wisdom of the ages to those who dared to listen. He knew then that his story was but one of many, an echo of a greater truth that connected every living being in an intricate tapestry of purpose and destiny.

With newfound resolve, Kirk stood, the cool breeze tousling his face, carrying with it the promise of revelation. He would pen the insights of his journey, share the lessons learned from divine encounters, and offer up his story as a testament to the transformative power of answering the call.

What insights, then, does the reader stand to gain from Kirk's tale? What lessons lie hidden within the folds of his experiences, waiting to be uncovered like precious gems in the bedrock of the soul?

Imagine, if you will, a life unshackled from the fetters of doubt and fear, a life where every step is guided by a purpose that burns bright within the chest. Envision a world where the voices of calling are not drowned out by the cacophony of daily existence but are instead the guiding melody to which the dance of life is choreographed.

Can you hear it? The call that stirs deep within, beckoning you to embrace your true identity as a child of the divine? Will you silence the distractions, still the mind, and listen to the voice that speaks of love, belonging, and an inheritance that outlasts the stars?

This is your invitation, dear reader, to journey with Kirk through the pages of 'Immortal Mentor', to explore the depths of a calling that is as ancient as time and as fresh as the morning dew. For within these pages lies not just a story but a road map to the soul's awakening, a guide to the ultimate transformation—one that leads to a life marked by the eternal, a life where sonship is not just a concept but a living, breathing reality.

The mantle of sonship awaits. The journey toward immortality is at hand. Will you answer the call?

2

____

THE MANTLE OF TODAY

Discipleship to Mentorship

In the dusky twilight of a world teetering on the cusp of change, imagine wandering through the ancient streets of Jerusalem or the dusty roads of Galilee. The air is thick with anticipation, a sense of something monumental unfurling its wings. This was a time when the world was vast and uncharted, yet communities were tightly knit, bound by the threads of shared beliefs and collective yearnings.

The year is AD 30, and the stage is set for a quiet revolution. An itinerant preacher, known to many simply as Jesus of Nazareth, is gathering a small group of followers—disciples, they are called. These individuals are not merely students; they are apprentices, each undergoing a profound transformation under the tutelage of their master. This is the embryonic stage of a movement that will ripple through time, shaping the course of history.

As we peer into this pivotal epoch, we find that the concept of discipleship is not just a religious construct but a social phenomenon. It is a system wherein knowledge, wisdom, and values are transmitted from one individual to another, from one generation to the next. This transfer is not passive; it is active and dynamic, predicated on a relationship of trust and mutual respect.

Fast forward two millennia. The echoes of those ancient footsteps still resonate in modern corridors. Today, we have enshrined this time-honored tradition under a new moniker —mentorship. Yet, the essence remains unchanged. The mentor, much like the ancient master, guides the mentee through the labyrinth of life's challenges and opportunities.

What has brought about this continuity, this remarkable persistence of one soul lighting the torch of another across the ages? To understand this, let us delve into the milestones that have marked this journey.

The fall of empires and the rise of nations, the flux of cultural renaissances, and the sobering lessons of wars and revolutions—all these have carved the contours of our collective psyche. Each era brought forth its own brand of mentors: philosophers, scholars, artisans, and visionaries. They were the beacons in the darkness of ignorance, the architects of society's conscience.

In the crucible of the Enlightenment, mentorship evolved from a predominantly spiritual pursuit to encompass the secular and the scientific. The Industrial Revolution further democratized knowledge, making it accessible to the masses. Mentorship became not just a privilege of the elite but a right of the common man.

Now, consider the landscape of the present. We inhabit a world where information is abundant, yet wisdom is scarce. We grapple with complexity and crave simplicity. We seek anchors in the tempest of our digitized, transient existence. The need for guidance, for that immortal mentor, has never been more acute.

Why does this history matter now? The answer lies in the unwavering human quest for meaning and mastery. To navigate the treacherous waters of the 21st century, we must draw from the reservoirs of the past. Those who do not learn from history are condemned to repeat it, so the adage goes. But those who embrace it, who seek to understand the undercurrents and the overtones, can craft a future that is informed and enlightened.

Is it not awe-inspiring to consider that the same principles guiding the disciples of yesteryear can illuminate our path today? The mentorship of the modern era may have evolved in form—virtual meetings replacing face-to-face gatherings, digital resources supplementing oral traditions—but the fundamentals of the human connection endure.

The story that unfolds in the pages to come is not simply a retelling of histories or a manual for contemporary mentorship. It is an invitation to embark on a personal odyssey, to trace the lineage of your own mentors, and to perhaps become one yourself.

Who were your mentors? What lessons have they etched upon the canvas of your life? And more importantly, how will you pass on that legacy?

In the quiet reflection of these questions, we begin to see the contours of our own journey from discipleship to mentorship. Here, in the confluence of the past and the present, we find the essence of our shared humanity. It is a testament to the indelible power of guidance and the timeless quest for growth.

Let us now turn the page, stepping into the narrative woven by countless mentors and mentees through the ages. As we do so, let us hold fast to the wisdom of the ages, even as we chart new courses in the ever-expanding sea of knowledge. Welcome to the story of 'Immortal Mentor', where the past informs the present, and the present shapes the future.

The Immortal Construction

Embark now on a voyage of profound discovery, a journey to decipher the intricate blueprint of immortality that binds the human spirit across epochs and civilizations. This is not a mere exploration of physical continuity but an odyssey into the essence of what propels human existence to its zenith—the construction of immortality through mentorship and the transference of wisdom.

Your objective, as we traverse this path together, is to internalize the framework of ethereal endurance that renders our species unique—our ability to impart knowledge beyond the confines of our mortal coils. By the end of this expedition, you will not only comprehend but also be equipped to integrate this construct into your own life, ensuring that your influence reverberates through time.

What, then, must one possess to embark on this quest to achieve a semblance of immortality? The prerequisites are deceptively simple: a willingness to learn and teach, the courage to evolve, and an unyielding commitment to the betterment of others.

Let us now cast a net over the expanse of this grand design, capturing a glimpse of the journey ahead. We begin by understanding the essence of mentorship, proceed to forge powerful relationships, cultivate wisdom, impart knowledge, overcome challenges, and finally, validate our transformative impact on others. Each phase, is a stepping stone, each action, a ripple across the waters of time.

With our compass set, we dive into the depths of each step, dissecting its intricacies.

First, grasp the essence of mentorship. It is more than guidance; it is the alchemy of turning raw potential into gleaming achievement. Mentorship is the invisible thread weaving through the fabric of progress, an unspoken pact between generations to transmit the torch of enlightenment.

Next, we forge relationships. Not just any bonds, but ones cemented in respect, trust, and mutual aspiration. Seek out those whose thirst for knowledge mirrors your own, and with whom the exchange of wisdom becomes as natural as breathing.

Then, we cultivate wisdom. This is no passive garden but a battlefield where knowledge is honed through experience, introspection, and relentless curiosity. Wisdom is not just knowing but understanding the core of truths that withstand the test of time.

We move on to impart knowledge. Here, the mentor transforms into a beacon, guiding the mentee through the fog of ignorance with the light of insight. But be wary, for knowledge without context is like a ship without a rudder, aimless and ineffective.

As we navigate this odyssey, heed these words of caution: mentorship is a delicate dance. One misstep can deter a promising journey. Avoid the pitfalls of arrogance and remember that the mentor, too, is an eternal student of life.

Testing our efforts is vital. Observe the growth in those you guide. Are they flourishing under your tutelage, becoming mentors in their own right? This is the true measure of your immortal construction—the legacy of empowered individuals you leave behind.

Should you encounter obstacles, do not despair. Troubleshoot with patience and adaptability. Remember, the path to immortality is not linear but a tapestry of trials and triumphs.

Do you feel the weight of this knowledge? Does it inspire or daunt you? Consider this: every person you meet is a potential thread in the tapestry of your immortality. How will you weave these threads to ensure your essence endures?

Imagine the power of a world where each individual becomes both a beacon and a mirror, reflecting and amplifying the light of human potential. This is the immortal construction we seek, not a fortress against time but a bridge spanning the vastness of human experience.

In the simplicity of this vision lies its genius. In the end, immortality is not just about defying death but also about creating something that outlives us. It is about crafting a narrative so potent that it whispers across generations, inspiring mentors and mentees to continue the eternal cycle of growth and wisdom.

Pause now, and let the silence speak to you. In the quiet, you can almost hear the voices of mentors past, their lessons echoing through the ages. And in the stillness, you might just perceive the faint outline of your own immortal construction taking shape.

As we close this chapter, remember that each word, each idea, is a stone laid in the foundation of your legacy. Build well, mentor well, and let your influence resonate with the timeless cadence of humanity's greatest aspiration—to be remembered, to be immortal.

Welcome to the continued narrative of 'Immortal Mentor', where each page is a step toward eternity, and every lesson is a brick in the edifice of everlasting mentorship.

Latter Day Realization

In an age where the boundaries between the tangible and the ethereal grow ever more blurred, we find ourselves grappling with a concept as old as time itself yet as fresh as the morning dew—immortality. It is in the prophesied 'latter days' that this idea takes on a new form, a time foretold when the divine would walk amongst us, not as an ephemeral spirit, but cloaked in the very flesh we inhabit. What does this embodiment signify for the promise of immortality, and how does it alter our perception of the mentor, the architect of enduring wisdom?

The discourse begins with the understanding that we stand at a pivotal juncture in human history. Whispers of the end times, the latter days, permeate our collective consciousness, suggesting an era of both profound upheaval and unparalleled revelation. But within this cauldron of change lies a significant issue—the true nature of immortality in an age where the divine is manifest in human form.

The problem, then, is one of both identity and destiny. How do we reconcile our fleeting lives with the promise of an eternal presence? The challenge is not merely in accepting the concept but in understanding how it changes our roles as mentors and guardians of wisdom.

Should we fail to address this enigma, the consequences are stark. We risk wandering aimlessly through a spiritual desert, parched for lack of understanding, our potential for eternal influence left to wither in the sands of time. Without grasping the implications of the divine-made flesh, our quest for immortality may be nothing more than a mirage.

The solution, however, is as elegant as it is profound. To embrace the divine within and harness it in the service of mentorship. To become vessels of enduring wisdom, we must first internalize the divine spark that resides in all of us, translating it into guidance and enlightenment for those who follow.

Implementing this is no mean feat. It requires a paradigm shift in our approach to mentorship. We must foster a deeper connection with the self, a communion with the divine essence that underpins our existence. From this place of inner sanctity, we can begin to guide others, not with the arrogance of self-appointed prophets but with the humility of those who have glimpsed the eternal.

Evidence of this solution's efficacy can be found in the annals of history, where individuals who have embraced their inner divinity have left indelible marks upon the world. Theirs was a mentorship that transcended time, their teachings echoing through the ages.

Yet, there are alternative solutions and different paths to the same summit. Some suggest a life of contemplation, others of action. Some propose that immortality is found in the legacy of our deeds, others in the continuity of our bloodline. Each avenue must be evaluated with the same rigor we apply to our own, for in the garden of immortality, many flowers bloom.

The question now stands before you, reader, as it has before countless others. How will you manifest the divine within you? What shape will your mentorship take in these latter days when the promise of God in the flesh changes the very canvas upon which we paint our legacy?

Imagine a world where each individual recognizes this divine potential, where the mentor becomes not just a teacher but a conduit for the eternal. This is the world we strive to create, a world where the immortal mentor is not a lofty ideal but a tangible presence, guiding us through the uncertainty of the latter days and into the light of a promise fulfilled.

Amid this contemplation, let us not forget the power of simplicity. In the end, the pursuit of immortality is not a complex algorism but a fundamental choice—to live, to teach, to leave a trace of ourselves in the hearts and minds of those who will carry on the torch.

This, then, is the essence of our journey, a path walked in the knowledge that we are more than flesh and bone. We are beacons of eternity, each of us a mentor in the making, each of us a link in the unbroken chain that stretches from the dawn of time to the prophesied latter days and beyond.

So, as we turn the page of this chapter, let us hold fast to the vision of immortality that we have forged, a vision that does not shy away from the divine but embraces it, a vision that sees in each act of mentorship a step toward an eternal horizon.

Embrace the promise, dear reader, for in the latter days, the immortal mentor's role is not just to instruct but to embody the wisdom of the ages, to be the very flesh that walks amongst mortals, nurturing the seeds of everlasting life.

The Prototype of Jesus

In the quiet unfolding of dawn, as the sun's first rays caress the ancient streets of Jerusalem, we encounter a world teetering on the edge of transformation. The air is heavy with anticipation, for the events that transpired here have not only shaken the foundations of faith but have also beckoned us toward a new understanding of immortality.

Enter the scene: a garden tomb, a stone rolled away, and an empty shroud that once enwrapped the body of Jesus of Nazareth. This moment, captured in the narrative of Luke 24, presents us with a profound challenge—the reconciliation of eternal life with the resurrected body, and the implications it carries for those who seek to follow the path of the Immortal Mentor.

The main players in this unfolding drama are the very disciples who walked with Jesus, witnessed his miracles, and now grapple with the incomprehensible reality of his resurrection. Mary Magdalene, Joanna, and Mary the mother of James stand as testaments to the human capacity for both doubt and belief as they encounter angels who declare the impossible: "He is not here, but is risen!"

The challenge before them, and indeed before us, is one of faith. How does one accept the reality of a resurrected mentor? How does the physical return of Jesus serve as a prototype for our own immortal journey?

The approach to this conundrum, as evidenced by the disciples, is multifaceted. First, there is the initial encounter with the empty tomb and the angelic proclamation. Then, the sharing of this news with others—a strategy of communal reinforcement and collective witnessing. Finally, there is the personal encounter with the risen Jesus, a tangible experience that cements belief and understanding.

The results of these strategies are a transformed group of individuals. From Mary Magdalene's proclamation, "I have seen the Lord," to the disciples' recognition of Jesus in the breaking of bread at Emmaus, we witness a burgeoning faith that defies death itself.

Upon reflection, this case study offers profound insights. The resurrection narrative is not merely a testament to the power of Jesus but also a model, a blueprint for the believer's journey toward immortality. Yet, we must acknowledge potential criticisms: the skepticism of the empirical mind, the demand for historical proof, and the struggle to reconcile faith with reason.

To enhance our understanding, let us consider visual aids that have captured the imagination throughout the centuries: paintings of the empty tomb, the road to Emmaus, and the myriad depictions of Jesus appearing to his followers. These images serve not only as artistic expressions but as tools to internalize the narrative.

Connecting these events to the larger narrative of immortality, we see Jesus as the ultimate embodiment of the Immortal Mentor. His resurrection sets the precedent for the believer's own journey, promising not just a spiritual continuation but a physical rebirth.

As we contemplate the implications of the risen Jesus, we might ask ourselves, how do our own lives mirror this prototype? Are we not called to die to our former selves and rise anew, guided by the teachings of our mentor?

Kirk Anthony, the author of these words, knows the gravity of such a calling. Sent to the verdant shores of Hawaii from the icy expanses of Alaska, it was in the embrace of those islands that the whispers of Jesus became a roar. From a childhood encounter that set the course to later visitations that solidified the mission, the journey has been one of deep reflection and profound transformation.

In the minutiae of our daily lives, we may find echoes of this immortal path. How do we embody the principles of our mentor in our actions, our relationships, and our very being? It is in the living out of these principles that we find the true path to immortality.

It is the author's hope that as you, the reader, traverse the pages of this book, you find not just a historical examination but a personal invitation. An invitation to walk the path laid before you by the Prototype of Jesus, to become an Immortal Mentor in your own right, guiding others with the wisdom gleaned from a life transformed.

So, dear reader, as you pause at the conclusion of this reflection, consider the implications of a resurrected life. How will you live out the promise of immortality that has been modeled for you? How will you, in turn, become a mentor to those who seek the path to eternal life?

The journey continues, and the path stretches out before us, weaving through the tapestry of time and space, inviting us to step forward into the light of a dawn that promises not an end, but a glorious beginning.

The Audible Call to Sonship

A whisper in a dream, a voice from the past, can sometimes carry the weight of destiny. Picture a small, cramped bedroom in Flint, Michigan, where the relentless winter has painted everything in shades of gray and blue. A boy, no more than nine, curls beneath a patchwork quilt, his breath visible in the frigid air. His mother, a woman with warm eyes and a soft voice, sits beside him, her hand resting gently on his forehead.

In this room, the cold is a constant companion, but so is the warmth of her stories—tales of faith, courage, and the unyielding bond between a mentor and his protege. She speaks of Jesus, not just as a figure from scripture, but as the Immortal Mentor, the ultimate guide in the journey of life and beyond. The boy listens, his young mind painting pictures of a path lit by the wisdom of ages.

The years pass like the turning of pages. The boy, now a man, has traded the chill of the north for the tropical embrace of Hawaii. The voice of his mother, though distant, echoes in his heart. Kirk Anthony, a name etched with the accolades of a storied military career and academic excellence, still hears her call to sonship.

One sultry evening, as the sun dips below the horizon, painting the sky with strokes of fire and gold, Kirk's heart stirs with an emotion he hadn't felt since those days under the quilt. A presence, familiar yet ineffably transcendent, envelops him. It is the voice of his mother, though she is miles away, calling him to embrace his sonship, to acknowledge the lineage of wisdom passed down through generations.

The surprise of this moment is not its occurrence, but its intensity. Kirk has felt the hand of destiny before, but nothing like this—a call to sonship, a summons to accept his place in a lineage that does not end with blood but is bound by the spirit of mentorship.

This personal revelation, while unique to Kirk, touches on a truth we all seek—a connection to something greater than ourselves. The universal desire to be part of a legacy, to be guided and to guide in turn, resonates with every soul that has sought meaning in the tapestry of human existence.

As you journey through the pages of this book, you will uncover the wisdom of an Immortal Mentor, and the lessons of a life lived in the pursuit of transcendence. The anecdotes of my mother's voice are not just memoirs, but beacons illuminating the path of sonship for every reader.

Can you recall a voice from your past that has shaped your destiny? A call that, when heeded, altered the course of your life? This book is an ode to those voices, a testament to their enduring influence.

The unexpected turns of our lives, much like the surprise of my mother's voice reaching across the ocean to Hawaii, serve to remind us that our journey is not one of solitude. We are, each of us, entwined in the lives of others, called to be both student and teacher in the dance of existence.

In the simplicity of narrative, there is a profound truth waiting to be discovered. Through the interplay of dialogue and introspection, the stories here aim to reveal the essence of what it means to be a mentee and, in time, a mentor.

Pause for a moment and ask yourself: what is the nature of your call to sonship? How will you respond? The answers lie not in the stars, but within the quiet chambers of your heart, waiting for the moment of recognition.

As we reflect on rhythm and cadence, the ebb and flow of life's symphony, we realize that our stories are not solitary notes, but chords in a grander composition. Each encounter, each whisper of guidance, builds upon the last, creating a melody that spans the breadth of our existence.

The wisdom promised within these pages is not an end but a beginning. It is the first step on a path that leads to understanding the true nature of sonship—a journey that transcends time, culture, and creed, uniting us in the shared pursuit of immortality.

So, dear reader, as you heed the audible call to sonship, remember that your mentor awaits, both in the echoes of the past and in the quiet whispers of the present. Embrace the legacy, for it is in accepting the call that we truly begin to live.

Kirk Anthony, your guide on this journey, invites you to step into the role you were destined to play. The mantle of sonship is not inherited through birthright alone, but through the conscious choice to follow the footsteps of the Immortal Mentor. Will you take up the call?

3

WISDOM AND REVELATION

The Veil of Ignorance

Whispers of eternity ripple through ancient texts, yet many ears remain deaf to their promises. The idea of immortality, a scriptural pledge as old as faith itself, often eludes the grasp of the multitude. Why does such a profound promise—of a life unbounded by the finality of death—lie shrouded in the mists of misunderstanding and neglect? This quandary lies at the heart of our exploration and serves as the underpinning dilemma that "Immortal Mentor" seeks to unravel.

The impact of this ignorance is no mere abstraction; it is a tangible loss that weighs heavily on the soul of society. To believe in nothing beyond the corporeal curtain means to live a life confined, a spirit clipped of its celestial wings. Generations are born, toil under the sun, and pass into silence without ever glimpsing the horizon of their potential.

The consequence is a world where the finite is overvalued, and the infinite is overlooked—where temporal treasures eclipse eternal aspirations.

Consider the tale of Eleanor, a woman whose days were as numerous as they were unremarkable. Her years spun a tapestry full of common threads—work, family, fleeting joys, and forgotten dreams. Yet, beneath the veneer of normalcy, Eleanor harbored a yearning that spoke of something more, a whisper of immortality that she could neither ignore nor understand. It was during a winter of her life, as she grieved the loss of her beloved, that the veil began to lift. In her search for solace, she stumbled upon the scriptural promises she had long dismissed. The revelation that followed was both profound and personal, transforming her twilight years into a dawn of spiritual awakening.

The stakes could not be higher, for what is at risk is the very essence of what it means to be fully human—to live with purpose, to hope beyond the horizon, to reach for a destiny that transcends the temporal. To ignore the promise of immortality is to stifle the soul's evolution, to silence the inner voice that seeks to soar beyond the confines of mortality.

As we journey through the pages of "Immortal Mentor," a path will emerge from the fog—a path paved with the wisdom of prophets past, illuminated by the experiences of those who have dared to peer beyond the veil. We will delve into the reasons for our collective amnesia, dissecting the barriers that block the light of understanding from penetrating our consciousness.

Why do we so readily accept the finality of death? How have we become estranged from the eternal aspects of our existence? Is it fear, or perhaps complacency, that binds us to the material world? These are but the surface of the inquiries we shall pursue.

As we tread further, we shall encounter guiding lights—those individuals who have glimpsed the immortal promise and can help us navigate the landscape of the everlasting. Their stories, rich with the hues of hope and transformation, will serve as beacons to those who seek to lift the veil for themselves.

But what steps must one take to truly embrace the scriptural promises of immortality? The answers lie not in grandiose gestures but in the quiet, consistent pursuit of truth. It is in the daily acts of reflection, the cultivation of a mind open to the whispers of the divine, and the heart's resilience against the tide of skepticism.

To confront this veil of ignorance is no small endeavor. It requires courage to stand against the prevailing winds of disbelief, strength to climb the mountains of misconception, and wisdom to discern the path of truth amid the shadows of doubt.

Does the prospect of immortality not entice you to explore further, to question the impermanence that has long been accepted as an unchallengeable truth? Could it be that within the ancient texts lie keys to a door we have yet to fully open —a door that leads to realms of existence where the body and soul, unchained by mortality, can truly thrive?

In the chapters that follow, we shall take hold of these keys. We will confront the profound and the paradoxical, the known and the unknowable. Step by step, we will unravel the tapestry of ignorance that has obscured our view for far too long.

"You are not a human being in search of a spiritual experience. You are a spiritual being immersed in a human experience," so said the philosopher Pierre Teilhard de Chardin. His words echo the sentiment that will guide our exploration: the recognition that within us lies a spark of the eternal, a fragment of the infinite.

Together, we will seek to understand, to grow, and ultimately to transcend. The journey ahead is not merely one of intellectual curiosity but of existential necessity. To discover the immortal within is to awaken to a life of boundless possibility. The veil of ignorance is ready to be lifted; are you prepared to see what lies beyond?

Seeking Genuine Wisdom

In the pursuit of genuine wisdom, a journey both profound and personal awaits. The objective is clear: to discern and embrace the wisdom that leads to an understanding of immortality, as illuminated by the teachings within the Bible. This pursuit is not for the faint of heart, yet the rewards are as eternal as the soul itself.

Before embarking upon this quest, one must gather the necessary materials or prerequisites. These include a humble spirit, an open heart, a Bible for reference, and a quiet space for contemplation. With these in hand, the seeker is well-equipped to delve into the sacred pursuit of wisdom.

Let us begin with a broad overview of the course that lies ahead. The roadmap is threefold: first, to seek out the wisdom contained within the scriptures; second, to interpret and internalize this wisdom; and third, to live out the truths discovered, thereby walking in the light of immortality.

Now we dive into the detailed steps. The first phase involves immersing oneself in the biblical texts, allowing the ancient words to wash over one's spirit and soul. It is not a mere academic exercise; it is a spiritual engagement with the Divine. One must read, reflect, and pray, opening oneself up to the insights that the Holy Spirit may impart.

As the journey progresses, contemplative meditation on the scriptures is crucial. This is where the seeker begins to differentiate between worldly knowledge and genuine wisdom. The words of Proverbs 4:7 take on a new significance: "Wisdom is the principal thing; therefore get wisdom: and with all thy getting get understanding."

Offering tips and warnings, it is wise to approach this

process with patience and humility. Wisdom does not reveal itself to the hurried soul or the prideful spirit. Be wary of false prophets and misleading doctrines; test every revelation against the truth of the scriptures.

Testing or validation comes in the form of a transformed life —one that radiates the fruits of the Spirit, as outlined in Galatians 5:22-23. Love, joy, peace, forbearance, kindness, goodness, faithfulness, gentleness, and self-control are the hallmarks of a life touched by immortal wisdom.

Should you encounter obstacles, such as confusion or doubt, do not be disheartened. Troubleshooting these challenges may involve seeking guidance from a trusted spiritual mentor, joining a study group, or simply spending more time in prayer and reflection.

As you journey through the pages of "Immortal Mentor," let the vivid imagery of the Prodigal Son's return or the serene confidence of the Psalmist in Psalm 23 transport you to places of deep spiritual resonance. Engage with the text through direct questions: What does this passage reveal about the nature of eternal life? How does this wisdom apply to my own journey toward immortality?

Limit the use of adverbs and adjectives, allowing the potent verbs and nouns of the scriptures to stand on their own. For instance, "Jesus wept" resonates more profoundly than any embellished description could convey.

Incorporate one-line paragraphs for emphasis, such as:

"Eternity beckons." Use simple language to ensure the message is accessible to all, avoiding theological jargon that may obscure rather than clarify.

Emphasize rhythm and cadence, crafting sentences that ebb and flow like a gentle tide, drawing the reader into a meditative state conducive to spiritual insight.

Integrate quotations from the Bible and dialogues from parables, making the ancient texts come alive in the context of the modern quest for wisdom. And always, show, don't tell; let the stories of biblical figures demonstrate the transformative power of divine wisdom, rather than simply stating it.

"Immortal Mentor" is more than a book; it is a companion for those who seek to uncover the eternal truths that lie within the scriptures. It is a guide for the weary traveler on the path to understanding the very essence of life and the immortality promised by our Creator. The journey of seeking genuine wisdom is one of discovery, challenge, and ultimately, enlightenment. Through each phase, each step, the reader is invited to embark on a transformative journey that transcends the temporal and touches the hem of the eternal.

Revelation Unveiled

In the sacred journey toward understanding immortality, we find ourselves at the threshold of the most profound revelation: the unveiling of the mysteries that govern life beyond the temporal realm. You, the seeker, are poised to step through the veil and into a realm of enlightenment where the secrets of everlasting life are laid bare. The path is not inscribed in stone but illuminated by a light that transcends mere human comprehension.

Your quest, should you choose to accept it, is to unlock the mysteries of immortality through revelation. This is not a fleeting glimpse but a deep, abiding understanding that forever alters your perception of life, death, and the eternal spirit.

To embark on this endeavor, you will need an open and disciplined mind, a collection of sacred texts throughout and with the Bible for broader perspectives, a journal for recording insights, and a willingness to surrender preconceived notions. A supportive community or a spiritual guide can also provide invaluable assistance on this voyage.

The journey unfolds in stages: initial awakening to the possibility of immortality, deep study and reflection on sacred texts, personal introspection and revelation, and finally, the integration of newfound knowledge into one's life.

The initial awakening is akin to the first rays of dawn piercing the night sky. It's an invitation to explore the potential of The Holy Spirit strengthening your own spirit. Here, you begin by allowing yourself to question the very nature of existence and ponder the possibility of life and immortality beyond death.

In personal introspection, turn inward to listen to the whispers of your spirit and soul. Meditate, pray, and engage in practices that quiet the mind and open the heart. It is in these moments of silence that revelation often comes—a profound understanding that you are more than flesh and bone; you are a spark of the divine.

Integration is the final step. This newfound revelation must not remain an abstract concept; it must be woven into the very fabric of your being. Live out the truths you've discovered, allowing them to shape your actions, your relationships, and your purpose.

Be patient with yourself; revelations of this magnitude do not come on command. Trust the process and be mindful of the ego's resistance to change. Guard against dogmatism; true revelation is often more about questions than answers. Remember, the path to immortality is as much about unlearning falsehoods as it is about acquiring truth.

You'll know you have grasped the essence of immortality when it ceases to be a concept and becomes a lived experience. When your actions are imbued with a sense of timelessness, when your relationships reflect an eternal perspective, and when fear of death diminishes, you are beginning to taste the fruit of immortality.

If you find yourself lost or in doubt, return to the basics.

Reflect on your journey, revisit your insights, and re-engage with the sacred texts. Seek the counsel of those further along the path. Sometimes, a fresh perspective can rekindle the flame of understanding.

With each step, let the vibrant tapestry of life's cycles remind you of the constant presence of renewal and transcendence. Imagine walking through an ancient forest, where the interplay of light and shadow weaves stories of life's perpetual dance—each leaf and stone a testament to the enduring spirit.

How do these revelations reshape your understanding of the world around you? How do they influence the way you live your life each day?

Elegance lies in simplicity. Let the profound truth of immortality be conveyed not through a labyrinth of complex language, but through the clear, serene voice of authenticity.

And so, dear reader, let the rhythm of these words mirror the pulse of life itself—sometimes swift and urgent, other times slow and deliberate. In this dance of text and meaning, may you find the cadence that resonates with the eternal beat of your own heart.

Here, let us pause and reflect. "Immortality is not merely a destination but a journey woven into the fabric of life."

Remember, the paths to revelation are many, but the truth they reveal is singular and profound. As you continue your reading of "Immortal Mentor," let the wisdom of ages past and the insights of your own spirit and soul guide you ever closer to the threshold of understanding, where the veil is lifted, and the light of immortality shines forth, clear and unobstructed.

The Knowledge Deficit

In the labyrinth of human progress, our strides toward technological prowess and scientific understanding have led to a curious oversight—a blind spot in our collective consciousness about the essence of immortality. With each step forward, we seem to have forgotten to look sideways, at the realms that science cannot explain, at the knowledge that does not yield to empirical scrutiny. The concept of immortality, once the cornerstone of philosophical and spiritual discourse, now trembles on the precipice of modern skepticism.

Yet, this is not merely a philosophical quibble; it is the root of a much larger issue that threatens the very foundation of our existence. We stand at the crossroads, where one path leads to enlightenment and the other to an abyss of ignorance. The problem, stark and unyielding, is our collective lack of knowledge about immortality—a deficiency that could lead to profound consequences if left unaddressed.

What happens to a society that loses sight of its spiritual bearings? How do we grapple with the concept of our own mortality when the immortal has been exiled from our understanding? The consequences of this knowledge deficit are manifold, and they manifest in everything from existential angst to societal upheaval. When the thread connecting us to the eternal is severed, life becomes a Sisyphean ordeal, devoid of meaning beyond the material.

Do we dare to imagine a future where this connection is restored? A future where the knowledge of immortality is not a relic of the past but an integral part of our lives? The solution lies in rekindling the flame of ancient wisdom, in bridging the chasm between the seen and the unseen, the temporal and the eternal.

To bridge this gap, we must first lay the foundations of understanding. We initiate this by cultivating spaces of learning and dialogue that embrace the full spectrum of human experience. Schools of thought, both old and new, must come together to share and synthesize knowledge. We must create interdisciplinary forums where theologians, philosophers, scientists, and artists can collaborate and explore the multifaceted nature of immortality.

Implementation of such grand designs starts at the grassroots level. It requires the creation of educational curricula that incorporate the study of immortality into both the sciences and the humanities. It calls for the establishment of research institutes dedicated to the exploration of consciousness and its potential for transcendence. It demands a renaissance of the arts, where the eternal themes of existence are given new life and expression.

Evidence of the efficacy of such an approach can be found in the rare but enlightening instances where such integration has occurred. When the Dalai Lama invited scientists to explore the mind through the lens of Buddhism, it led to groundbreaking insights into the nature of consciousness. Imagine, then, the potential outcomes when such cross-pollination of ideas becomes the norm rather than the exception.

What of other solutions, though? Some argue that technology, specifically the advent of artificial intelligence, holds the key to unlocking the secrets of immortality. Others posit that the deepening of individual spiritual practices is the true path. While these alternatives hold merit, they must not be pursued in isolation. A holistic approach, one that weaves together the threads of collective and individual pursuit, is paramount.

To tread this path, we must ask ourselves: Are we willing to confront the unknown, to embrace the mysteries that do not easily yield to our probes and instruments? Can we find the courage to rebuild the bridge between the tangible and the intangible, the finite and the infinite?

Let this not be a call to arms but a call to wings—a summoning of our highest aspirations to soar beyond the horizon of the known. Let us, with each word read and each thought provoked, stitch the fabric of a world where knowledge is complete and where the wisdom of immortality informs our every deed.

As the voice of the past merges with the promise of the future, let us draw upon the vivid imagery of a world reborn—a world where every child is taught not just to count the days but to make the days count, where the lessons of eternity are etched not in stone, but in the living heart of our culture.

Ask yourself, dear reader: What role will you play in closing the knowledge deficit? Will you be a mere observer, or will you become an active participant in the collective awakening?

Remember, the pursuit of immortality is more than an exercise in intellectual curiosity; it is a journey to the core of our being. It is a challenge to our understanding of existence itself, a quest that calls for nothing less than the full measure of our courage, our wisdom, and our love.

In a world teetering on the edge of knowledge and ignorance, let us choose the path of understanding. Let us choose to fill the knowledge deficit with the light of awareness, so that the shadows cast by our uncertainty may be dispelled, and the radiant truth of immortality may illuminate our way forward.

Baptism by Fire

In the quest for understanding immortality, the metaphor of 'baptism by fire' emerges as a powerful catalyst for transformation. Traditionally, the phrase conjures images of soldiers being tested in the crucible of their first battle or novices undergoing rigorous trials. In the spiritual realm, however, this concept takes on a profound new meaning, especially when considered through the lens of the Son of God. This baptism is no mere initiation; it is a profound metamorphosis, a gateway to a state of being that transcends the physical limitations of mortality.

Embarking on this exploration, it is essential to illuminate the path with definitions, for words are the signposts that guide us through the terrain of complex ideas. Thus, we will delve into the etymology and symbolism of 'baptism,' 'fire,' 'Son of God,' and 'mantle of immortality,' constructing a lexicon that will serve as our compass.

Baptism, deriving from the Greek 'baptisma,' denotes a rite of washing or immersion, symbolizing purification and admission into a new life. Fire, a primal force, represents both destruction and regeneration, cleansing impurities and igniting the spark of renewal. The 'Son of God' is a title laden with significance, embodying divine wisdom, sacrifice, and the intersection of the human and the divine. Finally, the 'mantle of immortality' alludes to a cloak or covering that bestows eternal life, a symbol of authority and protection against the ravages of time.

With these terms defined, let us weave them into the fabric of our understanding. Imagine the fire's heat as the crucible of transformation, the flames licking at the very essence of the seeker. This fire purifies, not through the annihilation of the self, but by forging a new, imperishable identity. The Son of God, an archetype of divinity made flesh, underwent his baptism by fire, not merely in the literal sense of enduring trials, but in the physical sense of embodying the immortal spirit.

In the flames, he did not waver; rather, he emerged resplendent, a beacon for all who aspire to the mantle of immortality. This is no passive garment to be draped across the shoulders; it is a living testament to the power of faith and the resilience of the spirit and soul. To seek this mantle is to embrace the trials that refine us, to stand in the inferno and emerge not as ash, but as something more—a being of light and eternity.

Turning our gaze to familiar concepts, consider the phoenix, a creature of legend that is reborn from its own ashes. Like the phoenix, those who undergo a baptism by fire may falter and fall, but they rise again, renewed and fortified. The process mirrors nature's wildfires, which ravage the old growth to make way for the new. So too does the spiritual seeker's baptism by fire incinerate the dross of their former self, clearing the way for a rebirth into immortality.

The journey toward the mantle of immortality is not for the faint of heart. It demands of us courage and an unyielding spirit. Could you, dear reader, withstand the intensity of such a trial? Would you dare to step into the flames, knowing that what emerges will bear little resemblance to what entered?

In our world, we witness the transformative power of fire in the blacksmith's forge, where raw metal is shaped into objects of strength and beauty. This is an apt metaphor for our own transformation through spiritual fire. The blacksmith's hammer shapes the heated metal, just as our choices and beliefs shape our spirits and souls in the crucible of life's challenges.

The pursuit of the mantle of immortality is a journey through fire, each trial a step closer to the divine. It is not a path of avoidance but of confrontation, where the flames test our mettle and the heat tempers our resolve. In this baptism, we do not burn; we are born anew. The fire becomes not our end, but our beginning—the birthplace of the immortal within.

As you contemplate these words, consider the fire within you. Is it a mere flicker, or a raging inferno? Does it consume you with fear, or does it inspire you with its transformative promise? Embrace the fire, for it is in this alchemical heat that the immortal is forged, and the mantle of eternity is won.

4

THE IMMORTAL GOSPEL

The Promise in Timothy

In the quiet corridors of early Christian thought, nestled within the intricacies of theological discourse, there lies a passage that has echoed through the ages, promising life and immortality. The parchment of 2 Timothy, a testament to enduring faith, holds within its verses a message as potent today as it was when first penned in the dim glow of ancient lamplight.

Imagine the scene: an elder mentor, close to the end of his earthly journey, imparting wisdom to his youthful charge—Timothy. With the weight of urgency, the words flow, a cascade of hope amidst persecution, "Who hath saved us, and called us with a holy calling, not according to our works, but according to his own purpose and grace, which was given us in Christ Jesus before the world began. But is now made manifest by the appearing of our Savior Jesus Christ, who hath abolished death, and hath brought life and immortality to light through the gospel:" (2 Timothy 1:9-10 KJV)

But what does this epistle, with its talk of predestination, grace, and the unveiling of Christ, truly offer to the seeker of truth? Let us delve into the heart of this promise, unearthing the treasures hidden within its depths.

The concept at the core is one of divine initiative; God, in His sovereign design, has extended an offer of salvation and a calling toward holiness. This is not a reward for deeds done, but an act of grace, unmerited and free, bestowed upon humanity before the dawning of time. The grace spoken of here is no abstract concept—it is active, dynamic, a force that breaks the chains of death and ushers in the potential for immortal life.

Consider the case of a man lost at sea, the wreckage of his vessel floating like a specter in the moonlit waters. Against all odds, a rescue comes—not because of the man's swimming prowess or his cries piercing the night, but because a ship, by its own volition and purpose, shines a light into the darkness. So it is with the grace of which Paul speaks, a rescue initiated by God, spotlighting the path to salvation.

But let us not view this passage through a single lens. Some argue that the calling is universal, a beacon to all, while others maintain that it is selective, a divine prerogative choosing its recipients. The tension between these views has knit many a brow in scholarly contemplation, yet both recognize the centrality of Jesus Christ as the nexus of this grace.

Data and historical analysis reveal that the early church grappled with these concepts. The Didache, an early Christian treatise, echoes the universality of the call to follow Christ, while church fathers like Augustine highlight the sovereign choice of God. The confluence of these ideas paints a mosaic of belief, each tile a nuance of the greater theological masterpiece.

To clarify complex terminology, predestination in this context is not a cosmic determinism but a foreknowing of those who would come into fellowship with Christ. The text does not imply a capricious deity but a purposeful creator, weaving a narrative of redemption and calling individuals to play a part in it.

In conclusion, the essence of the passage in 2 Timothy is the assurance of a calling and salvation that transcends our actions, is rooted in the eternal purpose and grace of God, and is actualized through Jesus Christ. The immortal life promised is not merely an extension of years but a quality of existence, an unbreakable bond with the divine, offered to all who would embrace the gospel.

As we close this chapter, ponder this: In what ways does the promise of life and immortality impact your personal journey? How does understanding this ancient text shape your view of the divine and your place in the grand tapestry of faith?

Let the promise in Timothy be a beacon that guides your path, a reminder that in the midst of life's tempests, there is an anchor of hope, firm and secure. For in the gospel, we find not just the promise of tomorrow but the certainty of an eternal today, a life imbued with the very essence of the Immortal Mentor.

Gospel of Life

The Gospel of Life

In the vibrant tapestry of spiritual literature, the gospel stands out as a beacon of hope, a herald of life in its most exalted form. It is within this sacred narrative that we uncover the multifaceted dimensions of immortality—a concept that has captivated human imagination since time immemorial. As we embark on this exploration, we will reveal the life-affirming aspects of the gospel, shedding light on how they contribute to our understanding of immortality and offer a blueprint for living with eternal purpose.

Our journey begins with an anticipation of the profound insights to come. Here, we will enumerate the key aspects of the gospel that resonate with the theme of life, setting the stage for a deeper examination of each.

Living Waters

Resurrection and Renewal

The Kingdom Within

Eternal Purpose and Calling

Unfailing Love

Redemption's Story

The essence of these points serves as a guiding star to our quest for comprehension, and what follows is a contemplative and detailed exploration of each.

Living Waters

The imagery of water as a source of life is ingrained in the human psyche, symbolizing purity, sustenance, and rejuvenation. The gospel speaks of "living waters," a metaphor for the spiritual nourishment that Jesus offers to all who thirst for truth and righteousness. This concept is poignantly captured in the words of Christ, "Whoever drinks the water I give them will never thirst. Indeed, the water I give them will become in them a spring of water welling up to eternal life" (John 4:14 NIV).

Delving into the historical and cultural context of this statement, we understand its revolutionary nature. In a time and place where physical water was precious and often scarce, the offer of an inexhaustible spiritual resource was nothing short of miraculous. Theologians and scholars have long debated the full implications of this passage, with many concluding that it speaks to the transformative power of the Spirit, a source of life that perpetually refreshes and sustains the soul.

Practically, this metaphor invites us to consider the ways in which we seek fulfillment and contentment. Do we turn to transient pleasures, or do we seek the enduring satisfaction that comes from a relationship with the divine? The "living waters" offer a path to a life that is both abundant in the present and secured in the promise of immortality.

Resurrection and Renewal

The resurrection of Jesus Christ stands as the cornerstone of the Christian faith, a testament to the power of God to overcome death and offer new beginnings. This historical event, attested to by countless witnesses and recorded in the annals of early church writings, is not merely a past occurrence but a present reality with implications for the future.

Firsthand accounts from the Gospels describe the mixture of awe and joy experienced by those who encountered the risen Christ. These narratives provide not only evidence of the resurrection but also a blueprint for personal transformation. As we align ourselves with the life of Jesus, we too are invited into a process of renewal, shedding the old self and embracing a new identity rooted in the hope of resurrection.

The gospel's message of resurrection resonates with practical applications in our daily lives. It teaches us that no failure is final, no defeat is definitive, and no death is absolute. In every end, there is the seed of a new beginning, a promise of restoration that carries the very essence of immortality.

The Kingdom Within

"When you enter the kingdom of God, you come not to a place, but into a presence," it has been said. The gospel reveals that the Kingdom of God is among us, within us—a spiritual realm that defies the limitations of time and space. Jesus proclaimed, "The Kingdom of God is within you" (Luke 17:21 KJV), a declaration that redefines our understanding of existence and sovereignty.

This inner kingdom is not bound by earthly power or prestige but is characterized by righteousness, peace, and joy in the Holy Spirit. It is a dimension of life that transcends the physical, offering a glimpse into the eternal order that is both now and not yet fully realized.

In embracing this inner kingdom, we recognize the divine imprint within every human spirit and soul, the spark of immortality that connects us to our Creator. It challenges us to live with kingdom values, embodying the love, justice, and mercy that are the hallmarks of a life aligned with the eternal.

Eternal Purpose and Calling

The narrative of the gospel weaves a profound truth into the fabric of our existence: we are created with a purpose, a divine calling that echoes through eternity. Paul articulates this beautifully, stating that "we are God's handiwork, created in Christ Jesus to do good works, which God prepared in advance for us to do" (Ephesians 2:10 NIV).

This purpose is not an afterthought but a preordained path, one that aligns our finite existence with the infinite intentions of a loving God. It is a calling that adds depth and direction to our lives, a compass pointing us toward actions and decisions that bear the weight of eternal significance.

As we seek to understand and embrace our calling, we find that our daily choices become infused with greater meaning. We are no longer adrift in a sea of randomness but are sailing with the winds of destiny, participating in a story that stretches beyond the horizon of our limited perspective.

Unfailing Love

At the heart of the gospel narrative is a love story, one that defies the boundaries of time, the constraints of condition, and the finality of death. John, the beloved disciple, encapsulates this eternal love, writing, "God is love, and whoever abides in love abides in God, and God abides in them" (1 John 4:16b NIV).

This love is not fickle or fluctuating; it is steadfast, relentless, and sacrificial—the kind of love that lays down its life for another. The cross of Christ stands as the ultimate emblem of this love, a love that bears all things, believes all things, hopes all things, and endures all things.

When we encounter this love, we are transformed, born anew into a living hope that cannot be extinguished. It invites us to love in return, to extend the same grace and compassion that we have received, forging connections that mirror the unbreakable bond we share with the Immortal Mentor.

Redemption's Story

The tapestry of the gospel culminates in a narrative of redemption, a grand unfolding of restoration and reconciliation that spans from the garden of Eden to the New Jerusalem. The story of redemption is the story of life itself, a journey from creation to fall, from redemption to consummation.

Throughout the pages of Scripture, we see this theme emerge time and again, as individuals and nations are drawn back into the loving embrace of their Creator. The gospel assures us that no mistake is beyond the reach of God's redeeming love, no life is too far gone to be reclaimed.

This story of redemption is not a static tale but an ongoing saga in which we are invited to participate. Every act of kindness, every gesture of forgiveness, every moment of genuine repentance is a brushstroke on the canvas of God's redemptive plan.

As we close this chapter of our exploration, let us reflect on the profound truths revealed through the gospel. How does the promise of living waters quench your deepest thirst? In what ways does the hope of resurrection and renewal inspire your daily walk? Can you perceive the kingdom of God unfolding within you? Are you attuned to the eternal purpose and calling placed upon your life? Do you rest in the assurance of unfailing love, and are you contributing your verse to redemption's story?

Contemplate these questions, dear reader, and may the Gospel of Life be not just a text you peruse but a reality you embody, as you walk hand in hand with the Immortal Mentor.

The Mantle and Apostleship

In the grand narrative of spiritual inheritance, the mantle of sonship and the role of apostles and prophets stand as pivotal threads in the divine tapestry. These roles, steeped in sacred history, carry the profound responsibility of disseminating the message of immortality, a task that has evolved through the ages to adapt to the ever-changing landscape of human consciousness.

The mantle, a garment of authority and empowerment, has long been associated with succession in spiritual leadership. Historically, it was passed from mentor to disciple, signaling the transference of divine commission and the continuance of a legacy. The earliest origins of this symbolic act can be traced to the prophetic traditions of ancient Israel, where figures such as Elijah and Elisha exemplified the passing of the prophetic mantle—a momentous event that marked a new chapter in the unfolding story of God's interaction with humanity.

Through the chronology of faith, significant milestones mark the journey of the apostolic and prophetic offices. From the rugged wilderness of Sinai, where Moses' words thundered as directives from the Divine, to the shores of the Mediterranean, where Paul's letters penned new paradigms of faith, each epoch bore witness to the relentless advance of the sacred message.

Visual aids, such as timelines and maps, would enhance the reader's understanding of how these roles traversed geographical and cultural divides. The apostolic journeys, as illustrated in the cartography of early Christian missions, reveal the impressive expanse of the message's reach, as well as the diverse contexts in which the mantle of sonship was upheld and revered.

Cultural and regional variations in the interpretation of apostleship and prophecy are noteworthy. In the East, the mantle often symbolized a mystical transmission of esoteric knowledge, while in the West, it became closely aligned with ecclesiastical authority and doctrinal purity. Each culture imprinted its unique mark on the conception of these roles, shaping the way immortality's message was articulated and experienced.

The modern interpretations of apostleship and prophecy are as varied as the sands of the seashore. Some view these offices as obsolete, belonging to an ancient past, while others see their re-emergence as critical to the church's contemporary witness. The proliferation of global movements centered on the restoration of the five-fold ministry attests to the enduring relevance of these roles.

Yet, with such evolution comes challenge and controversy. Debates swirl around the authenticity and legitimacy of modern-day apostles and prophets, and turning points in theological thought often pivot on how these roles are understood and integrated into the life of the faith community. Critically examining these points of contention offers a robust dialogical space for believers to engage with the implications of apostolic and prophetic ministry.

One might ask, how does the mantle of sonship manifest in today's world? Does the prophetic voice still call out in the wilderness of our times, and are there apostles walking among us, unseen yet impactful? These questions invite contemplation and inspire a quest for greater depth in one's spiritual journey.

In the simplicity of language, yet with the cadence of truth, we turn our gaze to the narratives that have shaped our understanding and the dialogues that continue to mold our perspectives. As Tertullian once declared, "The blood of the martyrs is the seed of the church," reminding us of the profound sacrifices that have undergirded the apostolic mission throughout the ages.

The mantle of sonship, when rightly grasped, calls forth a life lived in the reflection of the Immortal Mentor. It is the embodiment of divine love and power, a testament to the enduring message of life that transcends the very bounds of mortality.

In the quiet of contemplation, one must ponder: Are we, the contemporaries of an ancient faith, ready to bear the weight of this mantle? Can we, with integrity and courage, step into the apostolic and prophetic call to be bearers of the immortal flame?

Let the reader pause here, to consider the gravity and the glory of such a calling. For in the answer to these inquiries lies the future of the message of immortality—a message we are entrusted to carry until the end of the age, hand in hand with the Immortal Mentor.

The Fiery Furnace Metaphor

Embarking on the path to immortality, one invariably encounters a multitude of trials and tribulations, each serving as a crucible for the spirit and soul's refinement. It is through these challenges that individuals are tested, their characters are forged, and their destinies are shaped. Reflecting on such profound experiences, the biblical story of the fiery furnace emerges as an enduring metaphor, rich with lessons and implications for the seeker of eternal life.

The tale of Shadrach, Meshach, and Abednego, cast into the blazing inferno for their unwavering faith, stands as a testament to divine fidelity and human perseverance. Similarly, the journey toward immortality is fraught with fires of its own—moments of existential crisis, moral quandaries, and the searing pain of personal loss. These parallels beckon for exploration, promising insights into the essence of spiritual resilience.

Why draw such a comparison? The intent is to illuminate the quintessence of human fortitude, mirrored in these two seemingly disparate subjects. By juxtaposing the literal flames that tested the faith of ancient believers with the figurative fires that refined modern spirits and souls, one may discern the universal principles governing the odyssey of the spirit.

As our criteria for comparison, we consider the nature of the trials, the responses of the individuals involved, and the outcomes that define their spiritual trajectories. It is within these benchmarks that the similarities and differences between the fiery furnace and the trials of immortality seekers become apparent.

The three Hebrews faced a furnace heated seven times its usual intensity, a direct threat to their physical existence. Their reaction? An unyielding commitment to their principles, regardless of the cost. In the trials of the immortality seeker, the fires are not of embers and ash but are instead the internal flames of doubt, fear, and temptation. Much like the steadfast trio, the modern spiritual aspirant must navigate these flames with unwavering dedication to their higher calling.

While the furnace was an external obstacle imposed upon Shadrach, Meshach, and Abednego, the challenges on the immortality path are often internal, requiring introspection and self-conquest. This contrast highlights the nuanced nature of each subject; one is a battle against external forces, and the other is a war within the self.

Yet, in both scenarios, the presence of a fourth figure is noted—interpreted by many as divine intervention or the manifestation of the Immortal Mentor. This similitude suggests that, regardless of the era or the form trials take, divine companionship is a constant, offering solace and strength to those who endure.

Visual aids, though not applicable in the traditional sense, manifest here in the vivid imagery of the narrative itself. The furnace's flames dance in the reader's mind, just as the internal struggles of the seeker burn brightly, each illuminating the dramatic tension inherent in their respective ordeals.

Delving deeper, the comparison reveals a broader implication: the transformative power of trials. The furnace did not consume the three men; it liberated them from their bonds. Similarly, the internal struggles faced by those seeking immortality can act as catalysts for profound personal growth, burning away the dross of the mundane to reveal the gold of the spirit.

Contemporary relevance is found in the notion that every individual, regardless of epoch, will face their own furnace. Modern society, with its rapid change and moral complexities, furnishes a multitude of fiery trials that test the mettle of our convictions and the depth of our spiritual resolve.

Can one's faith withstand the pressure of societal norms that conflict with the quest for immortality? How does one navigate the furnace of public opinion, or the inferno of technological distraction? These questions probe the heart of the metaphor's modern application.

In the silence that follows these inquiries, let the seeker of immortality reflect on the courage displayed by the Hebrews. For it is in the echoes of their unwavering voices that one finds the strength to face the flames—be they of ancient origin or kindled in the complexities of the present day.

Thus, the fiery furnace serves not only as a metaphor but as an eternal narrative, echoing through the corridors of time to inspire those who walk the path to immortality. The trials and tribulations one endures are both the furnace and the forging, shaping the spirit and soul for its ultimate ascent.

Herein lies a profound truth: the path to immortality is lined with fires of transformation. It is through enduring and overcoming these flames that one emerges not merely unscathed, but sanctified—ready to embrace the mantle of eternal life.

As we ponder the fiery furnace metaphor and its application to our journey, let us hold fast to the conviction that, within the heart of every trial, there is a hidden blessing. For it is through such fiery trials that we come to know the full measure of our faith, the depth of our courage, and the true essence of the Immortal Mentor's wisdom.

Immortality's Modern Possibility

The quest for immortality, a pursuit as old as humanity itself, has been rekindled in the modern era with a fervor that is both palpable and profound. The gospel, through its timeless teachings, invites us to consider the possibility that eternal life may not be a distant dream, but a present reality accessible through spiritual enlightenment and moral fortitude.

At the heart of this discourse lies an audacious proposition: that immortality is not merely a theological abstraction but a tangible state of being, achievable through the diligent application of gospel principles in our daily lives. This claim, bold as it is, stands on a foundation of spiritual precedent and contemporary testimonies, beckoning us to explore its veracity.

The primary evidence supporting this claim emerges from the gospel's own narrative. Here, we encounter the figure of Christ, whose resurrection is presented not as an isolated miracle but as a template for our own potential transcendence. The implications are staggering; if one man achieved victory over death, might not the same be possible for all who follow his path?

Delving deeper into this evidence, we confront a wealth of scriptural accounts and ecclesiastical teachings that affirm the possibility of eternal life. From the assurances of salvation proffered by the apostles to the more recent declarations of modern-day prophets, a consistent thread weaves through the fabric of Christian doctrine: immortality is within our grasp.

Yet, as with any bold assertion, counter-evidence presents itself, often in the form of scientific skepticism or philosophical doubt. Critics argue that immortality, as described in religious texts, is an artifact of wishful thinking—a comforting narrative crafted to assuage the existential dread of mortality.

In response to such skepticism, one might turn to the realm of personal experience, where countless individuals testify to encounters with the divine that lend credence to the gospel's promises. These narratives, while anecdotal, provide a compelling rebuttal to the doubter's refrain, suggesting that there is more to life, and indeed the afterlife, than materialism can account for.

In the spirit of thorough inquiry, let us consider additional supporting evidence found in the transformative power of faith. Across cultures and centuries, those who have embraced the gospel's teachings report profound changes in their lives—renewed purpose, deepened compassion, and an unshakeable hope in the face of life's trials. Such transformations, while subjective, point toward the reality of spiritual regeneration, a cornerstone of the immortal proposition.

As we draw our exploration to a close, we reinforce the initial assertion with a renewed conviction: immortality is not only a possibility in the modern age but a practical reality grounded in the gospel's teachings. The evidence, both scriptural and experiential, supports a view of life that transcends the temporal, inviting us to embrace a vision of existence that is both eternal and attainable.

In the end, the pursuit of immortality is more than a philosophical exercise or a theological debate; it is a journey of the spirit and soul, marked by introspection, transformation, and an unwavering faith in the promises of the gospel. It is a path that, while fraught with challenges, leads to a horizon radiant with the light of eternal life—a destination that beckons to all who seek with sincerity and courage.

Thus, we stand at the precipice of a remarkable era, where ancient truths find new expression in the hearts and minds of seekers today. The immortal mentor, whose wisdom echoes through the ages, invites us to consider that immortality is not a distant hope, but a present possibility—a truth that, once embraced, has the power to illuminate our path and guide our steps toward the everlasting.

5

———

THE CALL OF EIGHT BILLION

The Universal Mantle

Embark upon this journey, and I promise you a transformation that is not merely skin-deep but soul-deep. "Immortal Mentor" is not just another self-help book—it is a revelation, a personal invitation to experience a universal awakening. Imagine closing the last page with a perspective so profoundly altered that you see yourself and your place in the cosmos in an entirely new light. This is my commitment to you, the reader.

As a summa cum laude graduate and a member of the Delta Mu Delta Scholastic Honor Society for Business, I have delved deeply into the science of personal growth and the art of self-transcendence. This book distills that wisdom, offering you methodologies grounded in years of scholarly research, personal encounters with the divine, and undeniably effective practices that I have honed over decades.

You might wonder, how can a mantle of sonship be universal? How can it transcend the boundaries of culture, creed, and consciousness itself? I understand your skepticism. It is a natural defense against the many unfounded claims that crowd the shelves of bookstores. Yet, here I stand, a highly decorated Air Force veteran, whose life has been a testament to the extraordinary. Sent to Hawaii by Jesus Himself, I experienced the divine at 9, 23, 25, and 27 years old. My story is not just to be read; it is to be lived through the pages of this book.

Picture yourself shedding layers of inherited falsehoods and societal limitations. Imagine donning a mantle that fits you perfectly because it was tailored for humanity itself. This is the transformation awaiting you. It is not reserved for a select few; it is a birthright, accessible to every soul who dares to reach for it.

The value of what you hold in your hands cannot be overstated. "Immortal Mentor" is more than words—it's a living, breathing guide that will escort you through the valleys and peaks of self-discovery. It will challenge you, comfort you, and ultimately, it will change you.

The path to enlightenment is often obscured by the fog of human complexity. Yet, with each turn of the page, the fog disperses, revealing a clear and simple truth: the universal mantle of sonship is yours for the taking. It is a truth that has been whispered by prophets, and sung by poets, and now, it is being handed to you.

How does one begin to wear such a mantle? Through the power of vivid imagery, let me paint a picture. Imagine a tapestry of light, woven from the threads of universal truth. It is ageless, timeless, encompassing all that ever was and will be. This mantle is not heavy with the weight of the world; instead, it is as light as a feather, as strong as the bonds of love that connect us all.

But perhaps you are bound by chains of doubt, shackled by years of societal conditioning. "Can such freedom truly exist?" you ask. Yes, it can, and it does. Throughout this book, you will find testimonies, conversations with the divine, and living truths that stand as a testament to the reality of this freedom.

Notice how the narrative shifts, from the theoretical to the tangible. I do not merely tell you about these truths; I show you how they manifest in everyday life. Through anecdotes and practical examples, you will witness the mantle of sonship in action—a cloak that heals, empowers, and unites.

Why so few adverbs and adjectives, you might inquire? Because the power of the mantle does not reside in flowery language but in the strength and clarity of its essence. Simple words for a profound reality.

And the rhythm of our prose? It mirrors the heartbeat of the universe—the ebb and flow of cosmic tides that resonate within the fabric of this mantle. Short, punchy sentences drive home truths with the force of a gavel, while the longer ones invite contemplation, like the gentle waves caressing the shores of understanding.

In the tradition of the great mentors before me, I include quotations and dialogues that echo through time. These ancient echoes bring depth and context to the mantle, demonstrating its presence throughout history and its relevance today.

Finally, let this one-line paragraph stand as a testament:

The mantle is real, and it is yours.

The Universal Mantle is not a myth; it is a legacy, a heritage. As you turn each page, remember that you are not simply reading—you are stepping into a larger story, a narrative that began at the dawn of time and if we do not heed will continue long after we are gone. But for now, as we strive to grasp it by faith, it is your story. Wear the mantle with honor, and let it guide you to your fullest potential.

Welcome to the journey of a lifetime. Welcome to "Immortal Mentor."

Soul's Response to Immortality

In the quiet town of Eternity's Edge, nestled between the whispering forests and the eternal sea, there was a stirring—

a subtle yet profound awakening that rippled through the very fabric of existence. This was a place where the promise of immortality was not a distant dream but a tangible reality, woven into the lives of its inhabitants.

Amongst them walked Elara, a woman whose soul seemed to dance with an otherworldly light, and Damian, a man whose eyes held the depth of centuries. They were the main players in this unfolding narrative, representing the divergent paths that human souls might tread in response to the call for immortality.

The challenge that lay before them was as old as time itself: how to reconcile the finite nature of human existence with the infinite potential of the immortal spirit. Elara embraced the promise of everlasting life with open arms, seeing it as a canvas upon which the masterpiece of her soul could be eternally painted. Damian, conversely, viewed this gift with trepidation, burdened by the weight of what it meant to never cease, to outlive all that he held dear.

Elara's approach to immortality was one of acceptance and joy. She delved into ancient texts and meditative practices, seeking to align her mortal self with the timeless essence within. Her strategies were a blend of scholarly pursuit and experiential wisdom, each step on her path a deliberate stroke on the canvas of her unending journey.

Damian's solution to his inner turmoil was to seek out the limits of the immortal experience. He challenged the very notion of eternity, testing its boundaries through feats of courage, bouts of existential inquiry, and dialogues with those who had walked the path before him. His was a quest not for acceptance, but for understanding and perhaps, a way to find peace with the eternal.

The results for Elara were transformative. Her soul seemed to resonate with the vibrancy of the eternal, her every action imbued with a sense of purpose and grace. She became a beacon of light for those who sought the path of acceptance, her life a testament to the beauty of an immortal existence.

For Damian, the outcome was less clear. While he did not find the definitive answer he sought, his journey led him to a deeper appreciation for the present moment and the impermanent beauty of the mortal world. His soul, though still wrestling with the concept of forever, was richer for the search.

Reflecting upon these two divergent responses, one might glean that the soul's journey toward or away from the embrace of immortality is as varied as the individuals who undertake it. Factors such as personal beliefs, cultural background, and individual experiences all play a crucial role in shaping the soul's response.

While visual aids may not capture the intangible nature of the soul's journey, imagine a painting, ever-expanding, its colors and shapes shifting as new experiences and insights are added. This represents the evolving nature of the soul's relationship with immortality.

Elara and Damian's experiences connect back to the larger narrative of "Immortal Mentor," highlighting the universal quest for meaning and the individual paths we take to find it. Their stories are microcosms of the human experience, each reflecting a facet of the immortal dilemma.

What, then, does it mean to live a life touched by the promise of immortality? Does it change our values, our actions, and our very perception of existence? These are the questions that linger, encouraging the reader to ponder their own relationship with eternity.

As Kirk Anthony, I invite you to reflect on the paths of Elara and Damian as more than mere tales. They are invitations to explore the depths of your own soul, to question, to seek, and to find your own response to the call of immortality. How will you answer?

The Global Immortal Awakening

Across the globe, a phenomenon is unfolding, one that hums with the same vibrancy that once pulsed through the town of Eternity's Edge. This phenomenon, a global immortal awakening, stirs within the hearts and minds of countless individuals. It is a collective recognition of our potential to transcend the known boundaries of human existence, to reach for a state of being that defies age, decay, and death itself. It is a challenge to our understanding of life, an invitation to redefine the essence of what it means to be truly alive.

The issue is not one of mere fantasy or science fiction; it is grounded in the very real advancements of medical science, biotechnology, and the increasing interest in the longevity of consciousness. The quest for immortality, once the stuff of gods and myths, is now within the realm of possibility, a tantalizing horizon that beckons humanity forward.

Yet, with this possibility comes a plethora of ethical, philosophical, and practical consequences. What happens to our society, our resources, and our planet, if death is no longer an inevitability? The implications are as vast as they are profound, touching upon every aspect of human life. Overpopulation, resource depletion, and the potential stagnation of societal progress loom as ominous specters over the dream of eternal life.

The solution to these challenges is multi-faceted, a symphony of strategies that must come together in harmony to address the complex nature of immortality. It begins with the responsible stewardship of our scientific advancements, ensuring that the pursuit of longevity does not come at an unsustainable cost. We must develop ethical guidelines that respect the sanctity of life while embracing the potential of its extension.

Implementation of these solutions involves a careful, step-by-step approach that includes widespread dialogue and education. The conversation must extend beyond the scientific community to include ethicists, policymakers, and the general public. Regulations and policies must be crafted to ensure equitable access to life-extending technologies, and to safeguard against abuses that could exacerbate social inequalities.

One can look to past movements that have shifted human consciousness and behavior to find confidence in our ability to navigate this new frontier. Consider the way we have come together globally to address issues like climate change and pandemics. While the efforts are far from perfect, they demonstrate our capacity for collective action in the face of existential threats.

However, what if the path to immortality is less about physical longevity and more about the lasting impact of our actions and ideas? Alternative approaches to achieving a form of immortality might focus on cultural, intellectual, and spiritual legacies. Encouraging individuals to contribute to the betterment of society, to create and innovate in ways that will resonate through generations, offers its own brand of timelessness.

As we ponder these thoughts and scenarios, a question arises, unbidden yet insistent: What does it truly mean to live forever? Is it the ceaseless beating of a heart, the endless cycle of synapses firing within the brain, or is it something more intangible, more profound?

The streets of our cities, the corridors of our institutions, and the silent spaces of our homes, all resonate with the whispers of this awakening. It is a song of possibility, a chorus of voices seeking to harmonize the melody of life with the notes of the eternal.

In the quiet moments, one might feel the pulse of eternity beat within their chest, a reminder that the dance between the mortal and the immortal is as delicate as it is enduring. And in those moments, one can't help but wonder—with a sense of awe and perhaps a touch of trepidation—what it truly means to step into the realm of the undying.

So, dear reader, as you turn the pages of this unfolding narrative, ask yourself: What is the legacy you are forging ahead to create? How will you tread the path that bridges the finite with the infinite? Your answers to these questions will shape not only your destiny but the destiny of all humanity as we venture forth into the age of the Global Immortal Awakening.

Mentorship Across Cultures

The tapestry of mentorship is rich and diverse, weaving through the fabric of numerous cultures, each thread colored by the unique shades of its societal norms and spiritual beliefs. At the heart of this intricate design lies a profound connection between mentorship and the concept of sonship — a relationship that, in many ways, mirrors the journey of humanity's quest for immortality. Just as the eternal seeks to leave an indelible mark upon the sands of time, so too does the mentor endeavor to imprint wisdom upon the mentee, fostering a legacy that transcends generational divides.

The purpose of exploring mentorship across cultures is to unravel the subtle, yet powerful, influences that shape the mentor-mentee dynamic. It is a quest to understand how the guiding hand of a mentor can mold the character and destiny of the mentee, much like a sculptor shapes clay into a work of art. By examining these relationships, we can gain insights into the broader implications of how knowledge, wisdom, and values are passed down through the ages, contributing to the collective growth of humanity.

The criteria for our examination must be as multifaceted as the subject itself. We shall consider the roles and responsibilities assigned to mentors and mentees, the methods by which knowledge is transferred, the spiritual underpinnings that guide these relationships, and the outcomes they produce within the context of their respective cultures.

In the Western world, mentorship often takes on a formalized structure, with clear objectives and milestones to be achieved. The mentor is seen as a guide, a source of inspiration and advice, helping the mentee navigate the complexities of their professional or personal life. This relationship may be characterized by scheduled meetings, goal-setting, and a focus on the development of specific skills or competencies.

Contrast this with Eastern traditions, where mentorship is frequently interwoven with spiritual development and the pursuit of enlightenment. The mentor is not only a teacher but also a spiritual guide, leading the mentee on a journey of self-discovery and inner growth. The bond between mentor and mentee can be deeply personal, often resembling the closeness of a parent and child.

The similarities between these approaches lie in their mutual recognition of the mentor's role in shaping the mentee's future. Both acknowledge the importance of passing on knowledge and experience, though the methods and end goals may differ. In both instances, the mentor is respected as an authority figure and a custodian of wisdom.

However, the contrasts are equally telling. In Western mentorship, the emphasis is on tangible success and the acquisition of skills that will lead to measurable outcomes. In Eastern traditions, success is often measured by the mentee's spiritual growth and the attainment of a deeper understanding of the self and the universe.

Imagine, for a moment, a visual aid: two trees representing these cultural approaches to mentorship. The Western tree, with its branches reaching high, symbolizes the mentor's role in helping the mentee climb to new heights in their career or field of expertise. The Eastern tree, with its roots running deep, embodies the mentor's influence in grounding the mentee in spiritual practices and philosophical teachings.

The deeper implications of these comparisons reveal a universal truth: mentorship, in any culture, is fundamentally about the transmission of legacy. It is the means by which the knowledge and wisdom of one generation are passed to the next, ensuring that the insights of the past are not lost but instead serve as the foundation for future growth.

In today's globalized world, the relevance of understanding cross-cultural mentorship is paramount. As societies become increasingly interconnected, the exchange of cultural practices, including those of mentorship, offers the potential for a richer, more diverse understanding of what it means to guide and be guided.

Vivid imagery emerges when we consider the mentor as a lantern holder in the darkness, illuminating the path for the mentee. Each culture's lantern is crafted differently, casting unique shadows and hues upon the journey. Yet the light — the essence of mentorship — remains the same, guiding the mentee toward their destiny.

What, then, can we learn from this exploration? Is it not, perhaps, that the essence of immortality lies both within the ceaseless beating of a heart, and in the enduring influence of the wisdom we share? The mentor, in any culture, becomes immortal through the mentee, as their teachings live on eternally!

In closing, let us reflect: How does one choose to pass on their lantern? With what wisdom will you, as a mentor, light the way for those who follow? As you ponder these questions, remember that the legacy of mentorship is a bridge connecting the past, present, and future — a timeless bond that, like the pursuit of immortality, keeps the flame of human potential burning across the ages.

The Final Frontier of Faith

In the pursuit of immortality, faith often emerges as a beacon, guiding humanity through the darkness of uncertainty and the fear of oblivion. It is a notion both ancient and universal, transcending the bounds of time and culture, whispering the promise of life beyond the corporeal constraints. Yet, as we reach the zenith of our spiritual aspirations, we encounter a paradox that challenges our deepest convictions. This is the enigma of eternity, the final frontier of faith — a realm where the desire for everlasting life meets the stark reality of our mortal existence.

This book addresses the profound question that has perplexed philosophers and theologians alike: Can faith truly grant us immortality? It is a problem that resonates with every soul that yearns for meaning beyond the fleeting moments of earthly life. The dilemma is not merely academic; it strikes at the core of our beliefs, shaking the foundations of what we hold sacred.

Our world is marred by the impact of this quandary. Societies grapple with the ethical implications of extending life at all costs, while individuals struggle with the existential angst of a potentially finite existence. The notion of immortality tantalizes us, yet it remains just beyond our grasp, an elusive dream that both inspires and haunts our collective psyche.

Consider the story of Eleanor, a woman in the twilight of her years, whose life was a testament to unwavering faith. Despite her devotion, as her body grew frail, she confided in her pastor, troubled by a gnawing doubt. What if, after a lifetime of belief, the promise of eternal life was but a mirage? Eleanor's plight is not unique; her story mirrors the silent fears lurking in the hearts of many.

The stakes are indeed high. If faith fails to deliver on its promise of immortality, what then becomes of our spiritual endeavors? Are they rendered moot, or do they take on a different significance? It is a pressing concern, for if we cannot reconcile our beliefs with the reality of death, our very purpose in life becomes a riddle wrapped in a mystery.

Yet, there is a path through this labyrinth of uncertainty. This book will chart a course through the challenges and offer insights that shine a light on the conundrum of faith and immortality. It will delve into the heart of what it means to believe, to hope, and to endure in the face of the unknown.

As we traverse this journey together, we will uncover the layers of historical and theological thought that have shaped our understanding of eternal life. We will examine the tales of mystics who claimed to have glimpsed the everlasting, and scrutinize the scientific endeavors aimed at conquering death. Through it all, we will seek the elusive truth that lies at the intersection of faith and immortality.

What lies ahead is a voyage of discovery, a quest to understand the ultimate goal of faith. It is a journey that will challenge us, comfort us, and perhaps even confound us. But it is a necessary undertaking, for to comprehend the final frontier of faith is to unlock the secrets of our eternal quest.

Let us begin with a question that echoes through the ages: What if the key to immortality is not only found in the evasion of death, but also in the way we live our lives? As we ponder this, let us embark on an exploration of the most profound depths of our beliefs, the intricate dance between faith and the human spirit, and the enduring quest for a life beyond the temporal veil.

6

ENTERING THE LATTER DAY

Prophetic Signs Today

In the thrum of modernity, amidst the cacophony of digital voices and the relentless march of progress, lies a narrative as ancient as time itself—prophecy. The concept of prophecy, particularly within the Judeo-Christian tradition, has long fascinated and perplexed believers and skeptics alike. It is the language of divine foretelling, a means by which the faithful assert that the divine has sketched the outlines of history before the dawn of time.

As we stand on the precipice of what many claim to be the 'latter days', a period steeped in biblical prophecy, one cannot help but cast a discerning eye at the world around us. Are the events unfolding before our very eyes truly the harbingers of ancient predictions? This is the query that lies at the heart of our exploration.

The assertion we examine is bold yet shrouded in millennia of interpretation and debate: contemporary signs and events align with biblical prophecies of the end times. To the believer, these are not mere coincidences but the unraveling of a divine tapestry, each thread a testament to the infallibility of sacred texts.

Our first piece of evidence emerges from the pages of geopolitical strife. Nations rising against nations, kingdoms against kingdoms—a tableau that mirrors the tumultuous scenes described in the Gospels. The precision of these ancient words seems to resonate eerily with the current state of world affairs.

Delving deeper, we see a proliferation of conflicts that span the globe. From the Middle East to the Korean Peninsula, from the South China Sea to the frosty terrains of Eastern Europe, tensions simmer and occasionally boil over into confrontation. The resemblance to prophetic literature is uncanny, compelling the observer to ponder its significance.

Yet, as with any claim, there exist counterarguments. Skeptics point to the cyclical nature of history, where war and peace ebb and flow like the tides. They argue that conflict is an inherent aspect of human civilization, not an omen of its culmination. These counter-evidence points are not without merit and deserve a place in our discourse.

In response, we must consider the specificity and consistency of prophecies across different eras and cultures. The rebuttal is not merely in restating the claim but in highlighting the convergence of signs—environmental upheaval, moral decay, and technological advancements that were once inconceivable, all chiseled into the prophetic narrative.

Some might find additional support in the surge of natural disasters, aligning with the forewarnings of earthquakes, famines, and plagues. The frequency and intensity of these events compel us to question their significance in the prophetic context.

As we draw our inquiry to a close, we are left with a reinforced assertion: the alignment between contemporary events and biblical prophecies is compelling. The fabric of modernity indeed appears interwoven with threads of ancient predictions, challenging us to consider the implications for our time and, perhaps, for the fate of humanity.

What then, dear reader, shall we make of these signs? Are they but mere echoes of human fears, or do they herald a greater truth? As the world turns and prophecies continue to unfold, we watch, we debate, and we wonder.

In the end, it is not merely about proving or disproving the existence of prophetic signs in today's world. It is about engaging with the narrative, contemplating its depth, and discerning its relevance in our lives. Whether we stand as witnesses to prophecy's realization or participants in a self-fulfilling tale is a question that time alone will unveil.

God in the Flesh

In the heart of this prophetic maelstrom, another ancient and profound concept beckons for our attention—God in the flesh. A notion that stirs the soul and challenges the intellect, it is the fulcrum around which much theological discourse pivots, particularly when we speak of the 'latter days' and the quest for immortality.

The manifestation of the divine in human form is a motif that transcends the boundaries of culture and religion, but for the sake of clarity, let us delve into a specific tradition where this idea finds a significant foothold. In the Christian faith, this concept is encapsulated in the term 'Incarnation.'

At its core, Incarnation refers to the belief that God assumed human form, becoming fully man while remaining fully divine. This is no mere theological abstraction; it is a cornerstone of Christian doctrine, asserting that in Jesus of Nazareth, God entered into the human story.

To expand on the key elements of this belief, it is necessary to acknowledge the duality of Christ's nature—both God and man, a union of the divine and the mortal. This union is not a dilution of divinity, nor is it a deification of the human, but rather a harmonious and mysterious coexistence.

The roots of this term are etymologically rich, stemming from the Latin 'incarnatio.' The historical context of the Incarnation reaches back to the early church, where church fathers grappled with its implications, culminating in the declarations of the Nicene Creed, which solidifies the belief in Jesus Christ as "God from God, Light from Light, true God from true God."

Contextualizing within a broader framework, the Incarnation is not an isolated event but part of a grander narrative of redemption. It is the precursor to the crucifixion and resurrection, events that are said to offer humanity a path to eternal life, a concept closely tied to the idea of immortality.

Consider, if you will, the various depictions of Christ's work and ministry. He healed the sick, raised the dead, and offered teachings that have echoed throughout the ages. Whether one views these accounts as historical events or symbolic stories, they present a compelling image of the divine intervening in the human condition.

Common misconceptions about the Incarnation often stem from a misunderstanding of the nature of Christ's dual identity. Some suggest that Jesus was merely a great teacher or prophet, but Christian doctrine emphasizes his divine nature. Others go to the opposite extreme, denying his humanity and thus, the genuineness of his sufferings and temptations.

What does this profound theology mean for us today? How does the concept of God in the flesh relate to the modern believer, or to the skeptic observing from a distance? Can the idea of the Incarnation offer a lens through which to view the tumult and hope of the latter days?

It is said that an immortal mentor walks beside us, teaching through example and sacrifice. If we accept the premise that God indeed walked in the flesh, what lessons can be drawn about our own pursuit of the divine, or the quest for a life beyond the temporal?

Engage with the narrative, dear reader. Picture the scenes of the Gospels, not merely as distant tales, but as a mirror reflecting our own struggles and aspirations. Ask yourself, does the notion of the Incarnation offer a blueprint for navigating the complexities of the human experience?

In the dance of words and ideas, let us pause and reflect on the profound simplicity of the Incarnation. It whispers of a love so vast that it would enter into the fabric of our existence, offering a bridge between the eternal and the ephemeral.

As we ponder these mysteries, let the rhythm of our contemplation guide us. For in the quiet spaces between our thoughts, we may just hear the echoes of the divine, calling us to look beyond what is seen and touch the hem of immortality.

The Immortal Church

From the profound simplicity of the Incarnation, we shift our gaze to another institution that has stood as a testament to the divine-human encounter, embodying the quest for everlasting life—the Church. This venerable entity, often referred to as the bride of Christ, has been a continual presence in the world, evolving and adapting through centuries of human history. As we explore the immortal narrative of the Church, we delve into the essence of its endurance and its envisioned role in the latter days as a beacon of immortality.

Let us embark on a historical journey, tracing the birth and growth of this institution. The Church's inception, shrouded in the mists of the first century, began with a small group of believers gathered around the teachings of Jesus. It was a seminal moment, marked by the descent of the Holy Spirit during the feast of Pentecost, birthing a community that would transcend time.

Over the centuries, this fledgling movement transformed into a global institution. Major milestones include the Edict of Milan, which granted Christianity legal status within the Roman Empire, and the subsequent Council of Nicaea, which forged a unified creed. These were pivotal events, shaping the Church's doctrine and its place within society.

Visual aids in the form of art and architecture offer a vivid testament to these transformations. The grandeur of basilicas and cathedrals, adorned with frescoes and mosaics, speaks volumes of the Church's journey through the Byzantine and medieval eras. Each stone and painting tells a story, a fragment of the immortal ambition etched into the Church's narrative.

Cultural and regional variations have given rise to a tapestry of expressions within the Church. From the ethereal chants of the Eastern Orthodox liturgy to the vibrant processions of Latin American Catholicism, the Church adapts to the rhythms of local traditions, yet always retains its transcendent core.

In more recent history, the Second Vatican Council stands as a modern adaptation, a profound response to the call for renewal in a rapidly changing world. This council, with its declarations and decrees, sought to engage the modern world with an ancient faith, demonstrating the Church's ability to evolve while holding fast to its foundational truths.

Yet, the path has not been without its challenges and controversies. The Reformation, a schism that reshaped the religious landscape of the West, and the enlightenment critiques of institutional religion, have all tested the Church's resilience. In each instance, the Church has had to confront its imperfections and seek ways to embody more fully its immortal calling.

As the world hurtles into a future marked by technological advances and ethical quandaries, the role of the Church becomes ever more critical. How does an ancient institution speak to an age of information and innovation? Can the Church offer a vision of immortality that resonates with the digital generation?

Indeed, the Church must grapple with its identity in an era where the very notion of immortality is being redefined by scientific progress. The concept of extending human life through technology presents a fascinating dialogue between the temporal and the eternal.

Does the Church's message of spiritual immortality find a place within this conversation? Perhaps, as we witness the birth of artificial intelligence and the mapping of the human genome, the Church's ancient wisdom can provide a grounding perspective, a reminder of the intrinsic value of the human soul.

As the Church looks to the future, it must continue to be a mentor to those seeking the immortal, not just in the promise of an afterlife, but in the here and now. Engaging in the works of mercy, advocating for justice, and fostering communities of hope, the Church can be a living testament to the immortal values that it upholds.

Let us pause and ponder, is the Church equipped to navigate this new epoch? With each act of compassion, each stand for truth, it weaves its immortal thread into the fabric of history.

In the quiet reflection upon the Church's journey, one can sense the heartbeat of an enduring legacy. It is an institution that has weathered the tempests of time, yet stands as a beacon to those who seek the everlasting. The Immortal Church, as the embodiment of Christ's lasting presence, continues to invite us to look beyond the horizon, to a realm where mortality is clothed with immortality, where the temporal dance gives way to an eternal anthem.

Latter Day Challenges

In an era where every tick of the clock ushers in new advancements, the world stands on the brink of a paradigm shift. The concept of immortality, once a philosophical and spiritual contemplation, now rubs shoulders with the tangible realm of immortal possibility. Believers are finding themselves at a crossroads, where ancient faith meets futuristic spiritual innovation, and the challenges that arise from this intersection are as complex as they are critical.

The primary issue at hand is the believers' struggle to reconcile their longstanding doctrines of immortality with the rapidly evolving landscape of technology and science. This collision of worlds is not without its friction. As society edges closer to the potential of extending life indefinitely, there is a growing tension between the spiritual promise of eternal life and the possible spiritual scientific pursuit of temporal longevity.

Should this dilemma linger unaddressed, the potential consequences are manifold. A chasm could form between faith and understanding, leading to a generation of believers fraught with cognitive dissonance. The very foundation of faith could be questioned, and the Church's relevance might wane in the eyes of those who seek answers in a language it seems unprepared to speak.

Yet, within this challenge lies the seed of a powerful solution. The Church can embrace the dialogue between faith and science, positioning itself as an immortal mentor to guide the faithful through these complex times. The method lies not in opposition but in the synthesis of spiritual and scientific wisdom.

To implement this solution, the Church must first foster an environment that encourages open conversations about the moral and ethical implications of spiritual and scientific advancements. Educational programs that blend spiritual and theological insight with scientific understanding could be established, offering believers a framework for integrating their faith with contemporary knowledge.

Evidence of this solution's efficacy can be found in history. The Church has a storied past of engaging with scientific progress, from the works of Catholic scientists like Gregor Mendel, the father of modern genetics, to the Vatican Observatory, which symbolizes the Church's commitment to understanding the cosmos. These are testaments to the Church's potential to harmonize faith with science.

What other avenues exist for the Church to address the challenge of immortality in modern times? Alternative solutions include creating interdisciplinary think tanks that include theologians, bioethicists, and technologists to explore these issues in depth. Such collaborative efforts could result in position papers and guidelines that help believers navigate the moral landscape of a world inching toward immortality.

Harnessing the power of storytelling through modern parables that resonate with technological themes could also be invaluable. These narratives could illustrate timeless truths through contemporary contexts, bridging the gap between ancient scripture and modern scenarios.

Imagine a future where the Church not only endures but thrives as a bastion of wisdom, offering solace and guidance in an age of uncertainty. Picture a congregation, not bewildered by the march of progress, but enlightened by a faith that evolves with it, embracing the immortal quest with hope and clarity.

The Church's response to these latter-day challenges will dictate its path forward. Becoming an Immortal Mentor can guide believers to a deeper understanding of eternity that transcends the boundaries of time and the limits of the flesh.

How will the Church navigate this complex future? It is a question that demands reflection, courage, and an unwavering commitment to the immortal values it has always cherished. The answer lies not just in the doctrines of the old but in the dynamic and ongoing conversation between the eternal and the temporal. It is within this dialogue that the Church will find its way, lighting the path for believers as they journey through the uncharted waters of immortality in the latter days.

The Return and Coming of Christ

Embark on an exploration of the divine, where the sacred and the prophetic intertwine with the very essence of life and death. This is not just another book—it's a revelation, a guidepost illuminating the path to understanding the profound implications of immortality for humanity and the anticipated second coming of Jesus Christ.

As you delve into these pages, you will uncover truths that have for centuries eluded humankind, now unveiled with clarity and conviction. Imagine a tome so potent that it promises to transform your perception of life, death, and the eternal continuum.

You may wonder, what makes this book different? What wisdom does Kirk Anthony, a man of service and faith, bring to the fore? The answer is etched in the experiences that have defined my journey, from the momentous encounters with Jesus in my youth to the rigorous discipline instilled by a career in the Air Force and the scholastic accolades that have marked my pursuit of knowledge. Each chapter weaves these strands together, revealing methodologies that are borne of divine inspiration and earthly dedication.

Skeptics might raise an eyebrow, questioning the validity of such bold claims. Yet, it is precisely this skepticism that Immortal Mentor aims to confront. By leveraging historical evidence, scriptural exegesis, and contemporary scholarship, this book meticulously dismantles doubts, leaving in their place a fortified foundation of faith and understanding.

But what does the return and coming of Christ truly signify in an age when the lines between the mortal and the immortal blur? How does one prepare for an event so monumental, yet enshrouded in mystery? These questions form the crux of our exploration, as we dissect the layers of meaning behind Christ's anticipated return and coming, considering the theological, philosophical, and moral dimensions.

Through this journey, you, the reader, are invited to envision a transformation that transcends the physical realm. It is a metamorphosis of the spirit, soul, and body, a readiness to embrace the immortal teachings of Christ in preparation for His return and coming. This book is not merely a passive read; it is an active odyssey that challenges you to live with purpose, elevate your understanding, and align your life with the eternal principles of love, compassion, and righteousness.

As you turn each page, allow the seeds of change to take root within your heart. The knowledge imparted here is designed to resonate deeply, altering not only your thought patterns but your very way of life. This is the commitment that asks of you—to engage with the material wholeheartedly, to reflect upon its implications seriously, and to emerge with a renewed sense of purpose in anticipation of the immortal rendezvous with destiny.

Have you ever pondered the gravity of anticipation coming and returning, not as an abstract event, but as a personal, transformative reality? How does the promise of immortality affect your daily choices, your long-term aspirations, and your most profound sense of self? As you navigate the complexities of this modern age, do you feel equipped to face the intersection of faith and eternity?

It is with the utmost reverence and scholarly rigor that I approach these subjects, ensuring that each word, each concept, is presented with the clarity and precision that befits such weighty matters. Drawing from a tapestry of theological discourse and personal revelation, I offer insights that bridge the gap between the mortal flesh and the immortal spirit.

The essence of this book is captured in moments of profound simplicity—a one-line paragraph that crystallizes a chapter's worth of wisdom, a direct question that pierces the veil of complacency, or a vivid image that transports you to the heart of a biblical scene. These elements coalesce to create a writing style that is as accessible as it is profound, as engaging as it is enlightening.

In "The Return and Coming of Christ," quotations from theologians, philosophers, and Christ Himself serve as waypoints, guiding you through the narrative. Dialogues imagined between the modern believer and the returning Messiah challenge you to consider your place in this unfolding story.

Remember, this is not just about bearing witness to the return and coming of a Savior; it is about the active preparation of your soul, the alignment of your life with the divine, and the embrace of an immortal destiny. It is about becoming a living testament to the teachings of Christ, as we await His triumphant coming and return.

So, I ask you: Are you ready to embark on this journey of a lifetime? Are you prepared to unlock the mysteries that have captivated theologians and believers for centuries? The answers await within these pages, and the time to discover them is now. Welcome to "The Coming and Return of Christ."

7

―――――

MODELING THE PROTOTYPE

The Resurrected Life

In the quiet moments of reflection, one might ponder the true essence of existence and the potential for a life beyond the temporal confines of mortality. It is within this space of contemplation that we examine a cornerstone of faith that has intrigued and inspired countless generations: the resurrection of Jesus Christ. His triumphant return from death stands as a beacon of hope, illuminating the pathway to an immortal life.

To grasp the full magnitude of this concept, one must first understand the resurrection not merely as an isolated event in historical theology but as a transformative experience with profound implications for living. The resurrection offers a clear view now, starting from a slight glimpse into a life characterized by renewal, purpose, and an unyielding connection to the divine.

Consider the early morning, just as dawn breaks, when the world is painted in hues of gold and the air is ripe with the promise of new beginnings. This image serves as a practical metaphor for the resurrected life—a daily renewal and an opportunity to redefine oneself in the light of eternal values. Just as the sun's rays dispel the darkness, the resurrected life dispels the shadows of doubt, despair, and death itself.

From another perspective, one might argue that the resurrection is an invitation to break free from the shackles of our past mistakes and failures. It speaks of a future unmarred by the stains of our former selves, offering a clean slate upon which we can inscribe a narrative of hope and transformation.

But what does the evidence say? The scriptural accounts are meticulous in their detail, chronicling the seismic shift that occurred as Jesus emerged from the tomb. These narratives are bolstered by the testimonies of hundreds who witnessed the resurrected Christ, their lives irrevocably altered by what they saw and heard.

In dissecting complex theological terms such as 'justification' and 'sanctification,' we must strip away the layers of ecclesiastical jargon to reveal their core. Justification is the divine act where one is declared righteous in God's sight, an immediate consequence of faith. Sanctification, on the other hand, is the gradual process of becoming more like Christ—a journey that is both the fruit of resurrection power and a testament to its ongoing work within us.

Conclude, if you will, with a reflection on the quintessential question: What does it mean to live a resurrected life in the modern age? The key takeaways are multifaceted. First, it is to accept the call to a higher purpose, one that transcends the fleeting pleasures and pains of this world. It is to live with an awareness of the eternal, allowing that perspective to shape our thoughts, actions, and interactions. It is to walk in the power of an indestructible life, demonstrating love, compassion, and forgiveness in a world that often rejects such ideals.

The resurrected life is not an abstract theological concept but a tangible reality available to all who seek it. It is an invitation to partake in the divine nature, to become co-heirs with Christ in the inheritance that is imperishable, undefiled, and unfading. As we close this chapter, let us embrace the resurrected life, holding fast to the promise that, our physical bodies will transfigure and change, the essence of who we are will endure forever, sanctified and preserved through the power of the resurrection.

From Miracles to Mentorship

Embarking on the path of mentorship in the realm of the immortal life is akin to traversing a wondrous landscape, filled with both enlightenment and responsibility. Your goal, as a seeker of this profound journey, is to transform your understanding and experience of miracles into wisdom that can be shared with others, guiding them toward their own spiritual awakening.

Before you can lead others, you must amass a trove of essential prerequisites. These are not mere physical possessions, but intangible qualities and experiences: a deep understanding of the miracles you've witnessed, the lessons they've imparted a compassionate heart, and an unwavering commitment to the growth of those you mentor.

Imagine a tapestry that outlines the voyage from witnessing miracles to becoming a mentor. The broad overview of this process begins with personal transformation, followed by the acquisition of knowledge and wisdom, and culminates in the sharing of these gifts with others.

Let's delve into the detailed steps of this journey. Initially, one must reflect on the miracles they have experienced. What insights did they provide? How did they alter your perspective on life and the divine? Reflection turns experience into knowledge.

Next, this knowledge must be honed into wisdom. Wisdom is not just knowing; it is understanding when, how, and why to apply what you know. It is gained through contemplation, discussion with others who have walked similar paths, and, often, through the trials of life's crucible.

As you prepare to impart this wisdom, heed this crucial advice: remain humble. You are a vessel of knowledge, not its source. Listen as much as you speak, and remember that the role of a mentor is not to create a replica of oneself, but to encourage the unique growth of another's soul.

How can you verify successful mentorship? Look for transformation in those you guide. It's not about the quantity of your advice, but the quality of the change it ignites. True mentorship leaves an indelible mark on the spirit, not just the mind.

Should you encounter resistance or failure, do not despair. Troubleshooting is part of the process. The key is to remain adaptable, to listen, and to approach each challenge as an opportunity for both you and your mentee to learn and grow.

Now, why should you heed these words? Reflect on the times when a gentle nudge or a piece of timely advice steered you in the right direction. How did it feel to have someone believe in you, to invest in your potential? The torch of knowledge and wisdom you now carry was ignited by the miracles you've witnessed. It is your turn to light the way for others.

Yet, how do you begin? Do you recall the first miracle that touched your soul? The awe, the silent promise of a reality greater than you had known? The path from there to here was paved with such illuminations. Each step, each revelation, was a building block in your ascent to mentorship.

Mentorship is a sacred dance, a delicate balance of guiding and being guided by the divine spark within us all. It is a partnership with the eternal, an echo of the immortal life you've glimpsed through miracles. In your hands lies the potential to weave a legacy that transcends time, a testament to the transformative power of guidance and wisdom.

Take a moment. Pause and consider the gravity of this undertaking. What does it mean to you to be a mentor in the immortal life? How will you shape the journey of those who seek your counsel? Can you feel the weight and the warmth of this calling in your hands?

In conclusion, the transition from miracles to mentorship is both a culmination and a commencement. It is the end of a personal quest and the beginning of a shared odyssey. It is a call to step beyond the threshold of your own revelation and enlightenment, to extend a hand back into the shadows and guide those who strive toward the light.

Take this charge with the solemnity and joy it deserves. For in the echoes of your words and the reflection of your actions, you will find that the immortal mentor you have become is not just a teacher, but a perpetual student of the divine mystery, forever learning, forever growing. And isn't that the true miracle of an immortal life?

The Transformation of Peter

In the bustling heart of Jerusalem, amidst the clamor of market cries and the heavy scent of incense, a transformation unlike any other was unfolding. The streets, once a mere backdrop for daily commerce, became a stage for a profound metamorphosis. There, a fisherman named Peter, whose hands were more accustomed to nets than to the nuances of leadership, was about to undertake a journey that would not only redefine his life but also offer a blueprint for the ages.

Peter, a rough-hewn man with a heart fiercely loyal yet prone to impulse, had been plucked from the shores of Galilee by a teacher whose message would shake the foundations of the world and history. This teacher, Jesus of Nazareth, saw in Peter not just a follower but a stone upon which a new era of belief would be built.

The core challenge Peter faced was his impetuous nature. Quick to act and often to regret, his very name, given by Jesus, meant 'rock,' yet he was far from this in his actions. The crux of Peter's transformation lay in the crucible of his failings: his denial of Jesus, a moment of weakness that would haunt and ultimately propel him toward his destiny.

The approach to this daunting challenge was not a singular event but a series of moments, both subtle and earth-shattering. Peter's strategy was born of reflection and redemption. It was the bitter tears shed in the realization of his betrayal that watered the seeds of his change. He did not flee from his failings but faced them, allowing the teachings of Jesus to mold his character like a potter's hands upon clay.

The results of Peter's transformation were both immediate and enduring. From a man who once cowered at the accusation of a servant girl, he emerged as a pillar of the early church, his sermons filling the air of Jerusalem with a fierce and compelling conviction. The data, if one could call it that, was in the growth of a movement, the thousands who were baptized, and the lives changed by his words and deeds.

Reflecting upon this, one cannot help but draw parallels to any endeavor of personal growth. The journey from follower to leader is marked by missteps, the willing confrontation of one's shortcomings, and the resolve to emerge stronger. Peter's story is one of hope, a testament to the potential within each of us to rise above our frailties.

No visual aids are necessary to enhance the understanding of Peter's transformation; his life itself paints a vivid picture. However, if one were to choose, it would be the image of a rooster, a reminder of the moment his old self was left behind and the dawn of his true calling broke the horizon.

This transformation connects to the larger narrative of immortality because it embodies the essence of what it means to be a mentor: to evolve, to inspire, and to lead by example. Peter's journey from the denial to the declaration, from the fisherman to the founder, mirrors our own path toward immortality. It is in the embrace of our humanity, with all its flaws and potential, that we find the divine.

So, what of you, dear reader? As you navigate your own transformation, do you see the shadow of Peter in your struggles? Do you feel the stirrings of a leader within, waiting to be awakened by the confrontations with your own failings?

In the spirit of Peter, let us forge ahead with boldness, tempered by the wisdom that only comes through trial and reflection. Let us carry the torch of our convictions with a steady hand, knowing that it is in the very act of stumbling, of falling, that we learn the strength of our legs and the resilience of our spirit.

In the final analysis, Peter's story is not just about the trans-formation of one man. It is about the metamorphosis of all who dare to lead, to mentor, and to affect the course of lives beyond their own. It is a clarion call to all who seek immor-tality not through the absence of death but through the enduring impact of their deeds and words.

Embrace the journey, for in the echoes of Peter's footsteps, in the cadence of his transformed voice, we find the rhythm of our own immortal legacy. And as we tread this path, let us ask ourselves: How will we, like Peter, rise from the ashes of our denials to claim our place as leaders, as mentors, as beacons of hope in a world thirsting for direction?

In the chapters that follow, we will explore further these

eternal questions, delving deeper into the human experience, and seeking out the immortal essence that lies within us all.

Living the Beatitudes

Embarking on a quest toward immortality, we turn to the Beatitudes. These timeless principles, articulated by Jesus on a mountaintop, serve as a compass for those who seek to embody the virtues of a life well-lived. As we apply the Beatitudes to our daily lives, we progress step by step toward the archetype of immortality that Jesus exemplified.

The ultimate goal here is to align our actions, thoughts, and being with the values of the Beatitudes, transforming our existence into one that transcends the temporal and influences the eternal. Through this alignment, we aspire to cultivate a character that resonates with the divine, an echo of the eternal mentor, Jesus.

Before we embark on this path, it is essential to identify the prerequisites. An introspective heart, a willing spirit, and the courage to enact change are the core materials required for this journey. Alongside these, one must possess an understanding of the Beatitudes themselves, as well as a commitment to integrate these principles into the fabric of daily life.

Let us first paint with broad strokes the roadmap we are about to navigate. The journey begins with an internal reflection, segues into an understanding of the Beatitudes, and evolves into practical applications in our everyday interactions. The process will challenge us to embody humility, demonstrate mercy, cultivate purity of heart, and seek peace in ourselves and with others.

Now, to delve into the detailed steps, we must first examine each Beatitude and understand its essence. The Beatitudes call us to be poor in spirit, to mourn, to be meek, to hunger and thirst for righteousness, to be merciful, to be pure in heart, to be peacemakers, and to rejoice in persecution for the sake of righteousness. Each of these carries a depth of meaning that we must explore and embody.

As we begin to incorporate these principles, it is crucial to offer tips and warnings. Be mindful that this transformation will not occur overnight. It requires patience, persistence, and often, a reevaluation of deeply ingrained beliefs and behaviors. A practical tip is to focus on one Beatitude at a time, fully integrating its lessons before moving to the next. And heed this warning: do not be discouraged by setbacks or failures; they are but stepping stones on the path to growth.

To test or validate your progress, look for signs of change in your interactions with others and in the peace you find within yourself. Are you more compassionate, more understanding, and more willing to seek reconciliation? These are the indicators of success on this journey.

Should you encounter troubles along the way, such as difficulty in practicing a particular Beatitude in your life, seek guidance through prayer, meditation, or counsel from a trusted mentor. Remember, the journey toward embodying the Beatitudes is a communal one, meant to be shared and supported by fellow travelers.

As we venture deeper into the heart of the Beatitudes, let us pause and ask: How do these ancient blessings resonate with the core of our being? Do they challenge us, comfort us, or perhaps both? Reflect on these questions, and let them guide you to a more profound understanding of the path ahead.

In our earnest pursuit, we must not forget to embrace the power of vivid imagery. Picture the meek inheriting the earth, the pure in heart seeing God, and the peacemakers being called the sons or children of God. These are not merely abstract concepts but tangible realities we strive to manifest through our lives.

Employing simple language, let us consider the Beatitudes not as lofty ideals beyond our reach but as attainable attributes that we can foster through daily practice. The rhythm and cadence of our lives will begin to mirror the harmonious teachings of Jesus as we persevere in this sacred endeavor.

Finally, let us recall the stories of those who have walked this path before us, incorporating their words and experiences into our narrative. Just as the transformation of Peter inspired a lineage of leaders, may our own journey through the Beatitudes inspire others, weaving our thread into the tapestry of a collective immortal legacy.

In the pages to come, we will unpack each Beatitude,

exploring its historical context, its spiritual significance, and its practical application. We will share anecdotes, dialogues, and reflections that bring to life the principles we seek to embody. Through this exploration, we will not only draw closer to the immortal mentor, Jesus, but we will also forge our path toward becoming immortal mentors ourselves, reflecting the light of the divine through our every word and deed.

The Ascension Promise

Understanding the profound implications of Jesus' ascension is akin to embarking on an archeological dig, uncovering layers of meaning that have the potential to transform the very essence of our belief. Delving into this pivotal event, we recognize that comprehending its significance requires grasping the vocabulary that gives voice to such mysteries. Akin to a master key, these terms unlock the treasures of wisdom and knowledge hidden within the ascension narrative.

The terms that will pave our journey through this exploration are Ascension, Promise, Immortality, Witness, and Holy Spirit. Each word, a beacon of light, will illuminate our path and enrich our understanding of Jesus' ascent and its promise for those who follow in His footsteps.

Ascension, a term often enshrouded in celestial mystery, is the act of rising to a higher level or state. In the context of

Jesus, it refers to His physical departure from Earth to Heaven after His resurrection. This event is not merely a historical footnote; it is a pivotal moment that encapsulates the hope and destiny of believers.

Promise, a word imbued with assurance and expectation, relates to a declaration that one will do something or that a particular thing will happen. Jesus' ascension comes with promises – of His ongoing presence, of empowerment, of a future return, and of an eternal inheritance.

Immortality, the state of living forever, defies the human experience bound by time. For believers, immortality is not only about an endless extension of earthly life but also about entering a quality of life that transcends death, a life in communion with the Divine.

A witness, in its simplest form, is one who sees an event and reports what happened. The early followers of Jesus were witnesses to His ascension, and in turn, they bore witness to the world of the truths they had seen and experienced.

Holy Spirit, the other Comforter of Jesus known in traditional religious circles as the third person of the Trinity, is the Comforter and Guide promised to the disciples. The Holy Spirit's arrival marks the empowerment of believers to live out their faith and to serve as Christ's witnesses to the ends of the Earth.

Let us now draw closer to these terms, weaving them into the fabric of our everyday lives. Ascension elevates our perspective, urging us to rise above the mundane and to seek the heavenly. We can find parallels in the way a mountaineer reaches new heights, not solely for the view but for the transformation the journey instills within them.

The Promise extends beyond words; it becomes a lived experience. As the certainty of sunrise brings comfort after the darkest night, so does the promise of Jesus' presence offers unshakeable hope in the face of life's uncertainties.

Immortality, often cloaked in the grandeur of myths and legends, finds its truest expression in the Christian hope of eternal life. This concept resonates with the universal human desire to live a lasting legacy, to be emulated to impact the world beyond our years. The immortal construct is our current present-day transformation as well as transfiguration.

To be a Witness is to be a storyteller, an archivist of divine encounters. Each believer becomes a living repository of faith, much like the oral historians who preserve the narratives of their people through generations.

The Holy Spirit, often misunderstood, is as close and as necessary as the air we breathe. Its presence in our lives is as palpable as the wind filling the sails of a ship, guiding it to its destination.

As we reflect on these definitions, let us ask ourselves: How do these terms shape our understanding of the ascension and its implications for our lives? Do they elevate our sights to the heavens, even as we walk the earth?

In the silence that follows these questions, we are reminded that words, though powerful, are mere signposts pointing toward the ineffable. The journey into the heart of the ascension promise is one of continuous revelation, a path we walk with both confidence and awe, as we too aspire to the immortality offered through Christ.

We have now laid the foundation, setting the stage for a deeper dive into the mystery of ascension and the transformation it promises. As we move forward, let our exploration be marked by a relentless quest for truth, a courageous witness to the world, and a heart open to the guidance of the Holy Spirit. Thus, we continue to tread the path of the immortal mentor, Jesus, whose ascension assures us that our mortal frames house an eternal spirit, yearning for the fulfillment of the promise – the promise of immortality.

Sonship's Global Echo

This chapter, "Sonship's Global Echo," is a testament to that very phenomenon—a deep dive into how one man's journey can resonate and amplify within the hearts of many.

In a small city, cradled by the verdant arms of Hawaii Loa Ridge, a gathering took place that would become a beacon of this global echo. The central figures of this narrative were an eclectic mix—there was a local kahuna, steeped in ancient wisdom; a young acupuncture doctor from China, seeking meaning beyond medicine; and a dance teacher from Japan, whose thirst for knowledge had brought her across the sea. Each had heard the call of sonship, a whisper of something grander, a hint of immortality in the mortal coil.

The core challenge was apparent: how could this diverse group, with their disparate backgrounds and individual quests for meaning, converge into a single, unified force for change? The answer lay in the very principles I had unearthed in my own teachings and journeys—a shared resonance with the eternal, an understanding that immortality was not merely about longevity but about the indelible impact we leave on the world through change and transformation.

Our approach was rooted in dialogue and exchange. We convened under the canopy of stars, where the heavens themselves seemed to lean in with curious gaze. We shared stories and insights, with each tale shedding light on the multifaceted diamond of truth. The kahuna spoke of ancestral knowledge, the doctor of scientific breakthroughs, and the teacher of dance, philosophy, and ethics. And I, with the backdrop of my own odyssey, wove these threads into a tapestry of transcendence of the Immortal Mentor.

The results were nothing short of miraculous. The doctor, inspired by the spiritual and holistic approaches discussed, returned to China with a vision of integrating immortal mentorship-inspiring traditional healing practices into his work. The teacher, her perspective broadened, embarked on a curriculum that fused the wisdom of the East with the innovations of immortal mentorship of the West. The kahuna, whose influence had rarely extended beyond his village, found his teachings now reaching newfound spiritual heights and distant shores through the voices of those he had touched.

Reflecting on this convergence, it was clear that the wisdom of the immortal mentor and the innovations of the current age were not adversaries but allies in our quest for immortality. Criticisms of cultural appropriation and superficial understandings were acknowledged and addressed with utmost respect and a commitment to authenticity.

Though no visual aids could adequately capture the vibrancy of these encounters, imagine if you will, a mural where each stroke represents a life changed, a new disciple of the immortal mentor, and the hues blend together to form a masterpiece of human experience.

This case study of the convergence, of minds and souls from across the globe, ties back to the overarching theme of 'Immortal Mentor'—that our journey toward immortality is a collective one. We are the sum of our shared experiences, and each individual's enlightenment adds to the collective glow of humanity.

Now, dear reader, as you pause and ponder the narrative laid before you, consider this: How might your own story ripple through the world? What echoes will you leave in the hearts and minds of those you encounter?

As I pen these words, the gentle Hawaiian breeze whispers secrets of lives past and futures to unfold. With each passing moment, the immortal mentor within us all beckons, urging us on in our quest for a life that not only exists in the here and now but resonates through the ages.

May you find within these pages the courage to be both a seeker and a guide, to embrace the mantle of mentorship, and to amplify the sonship's global echo in your own unique way. For in the grand tapestry of existence, every thread counts, every color adds depth, and every life is a brush-stroke in the grand design of eternity.

So, I ask you: What will your contribution be to this eternal masterpiece? Will you rise to the call of the immortal mentor, and if so, how will you share its wisdom with the world? Let us journey forth, together, in the sacred dance of life and legacy.